Amazon Reviews

Reviews from a previous edition of this book titled "Rules of Engagement" by Jerry McColgin

"A lot of the books we read come off as impractical and unrealistic in a lot of ways. McColgin's book was the exact opposite and exactly what we were looking for! In it, he shares a ton of stories from his own life which makes the book instantly relatable. He doesn't come off as a pretentious "expert" who has a perfect marriage, but more as a friend… God's design for our marriage is obviously a foundation, but the book doesn't come off preachy or guilt-inducing. Overall, I would recommend this book for any married couple. It made us laugh, think and even want to cry at times. This is exactly what we were looking for as we continue to build a strong, Godly marriage!"

—D. Sweeney

This is a book that I enjoyed reading and gave me ideas on how to improve my marriage of 36 years. It's timely in that I will give to my daughter and son-in-law who are getting married this weekend, as well as our son and his wife, who have been married for almost 10 years. Easy to read with thoughtful content and excellent ideas for strengthening a marriage. Suitable to read for yourself, as a couple or for small group discussion.

—J. Geary

"What an excellent book! God did not design marriage to be dull or boring. Unfortunately, however, our culture continues to paint marriage in such a negative light. In Rules of Engagement, Jerry McColgin shares practical insights from his own marriage and years of marriage ministry that can help all couples, whether newlyweds or 50-year veterans, to have the beautiful, fulfilling marriage God had in mind..."

—J. Motsinger

"The author opens up his heart in this book to show how he keeps his sustaining love with his wife through faith. I highly recommend this book to married couples of all ages so that they can recognize what humor, pitfalls, challenges and everlasting love can bring to all marriages. His marital rules are defined with real-life stories and scripture which provide an attainable infrastructure for all wedded couples."

—Amazon Customer

"Full of practical suggestions and Biblical wisdom, this book is an easy and engaging read. The author provides thoughtful material to not only spark discussions with your spouse, but also to excite you about what your marriage could and should be. The real-life examples used are not extremes - they are relatable and easily identifiable as common struggles faced by most couples which can be overcome with intentionality and direction from the creator of marriage, God. I was looking for a book to excite me about building up and strengthening my marriage and this book was a great fit!"

—J. Roberts

SHOCKING MARRIAGE

SHOCKING MARRIAGE

Transforming Complacency by Proactively Refocusing, Protecting & Reinvigorating Your Relationship

JERRY MCCOLGIN

Printed in the United States of America

Published by Author Academy Elite
PO Box 43, Powell, OH 43035
www.AuthorAcademyElite.com

Identifiers:
Library of Congress Control Number: 2020920601
ISBN: 978-1-64746-572-8 (paperback)
ISBN: 978-1-64746-573-5 (hardback)
ISBN: 978-1-64746-574-2 (ebook)

Dedication

To my parents, who in their seventy plus years together showed me what is was like to truly have a shocking marriage

CONTENTS

INTRODUCTION   IX

PART 1: REFOCUS YOUR MARRIAGE

CHAPTER 1: DESIRE A SHOCKING MARRIAGE   3

CHAPTER 2: BUILD A SOLID FOUNDATION   18

PART 2: PROTECT YOUR MARRIAGE

CHAPTER 3: RULES OF ENGAGEMENT - FRAMEWORK   39

CHAPTER 4: DEALING WITH CONFLICT   50

CHAPTER 5: WEATHERING LIFE'S STORMS   71

CHAPTER 6: OUTSIDE INFLUENCES   87

PART 3: REINVIGORATE YOUR MARRIAGE

CHAPTER 7: KEEP THE SPARK ALIVE   105

CHAPTER 8: PHYSICAL INTIMACY   121

CHAPTER 9: MODELING YOUR MARRIAGE   138

CHAPTER 10: EFFECTIVE COMMUNICATION   152

LEADER'S STUDY GUIDE FOR SMALL GROUPS   165

ABOUT THE AUTHOR   175

INTRODUCTION

Marriage should be the most unique and wonderful relationship you can experience. Unfortunately for many couples, reality falls quite short of initial expectations. With the distractions and pressures of everyday life, many couples don't even realize their marriage is suffering. Over time they've come to accept things as they are, settling for far less than what could be or what was intended.

Personally, I love marriage and I love being married. It grieves me when I see people just going through the motions or living as a roommate with their spouse. My wife, Tara, and I have created and conducted workshops and coached individual couples in an effort to improve marriages. Over the course of doing so, we have seen many couples evolve from boredom to joy. God has given me a calling – to help couples overcome mediocrity and strive for something more – a truly Shocking Marriage!

I am not your typical marriage pastor, if there is such a thing. I am an engineer by training and have spent the bulk of my professional life developing new products and making processes more efficient. I began my career in a washing machine factory then worked my way up in corporate life to the point of running major global projects. After that, I left to start my own consulting business focused on strategy and innovation. My customers were large consumer product companies. Many were once leaders in the market but over time their products had become tired and lost their uniqueness. The service I provided was to figure out why these products were no longer relevant and to suggest changes that would put them back on top again. To accomplish this, I spent time with consumers who used the products and uncovered their unmet, sometimes unspoken needs. With that understanding, I would help companies either modify their existing products or develop new products that could satisfy the needs of their target market.

Even while leading that business for nearly two decades, I began to feel God calling me to speak into marriages. I started by writing the Shocking Marriage blog in my spare time. Eventually, He made it clear He wanted more from me in this area. I obeyed God's call, became ordained as a Christian minister and shifted my focus to full time marriage coaching and ministry.

I came to realize my approach to improving marriages was not radically different than my efforts in resuscitating tired products. Analyze and understand the current state of the product (relationship), gain a deep understanding of the customer's (spouse's) unmet needs, and develop enhancements (guidelines) that will rejuvenate the product (marriage).

Our marriage is not perfect; no marriage is. But our track record is strong. As of the writing of this book, we have completed our thirty-eighth year of marriage. I can honestly say that in many ways, year thirty-eight has been the best one yet. We both come from long lines of successful marriages. At the time of my mother's death, my parents had been married for over seventy years! Likewise, when Tara's dad passed away, her parents had been married for fifty-six. I have three older brothers who collectively share over 140 years of marriage. There has been no divorce in either of our lineages as far back as we can see. I don't write this to boast or to imply we are special in any way. But just as a master carpenter will share tips and techniques to an apprentice, there are behaviors and attitudes that we can share to help you enhance your own marriage.

Here's the reality, all couples go through trials in their marriage. Marriages that fail in managing these trials often end up in dysfunction or divorce. Others may survive such trials but end up facing the same trials repeatedly by failing to learn from them. Marriages that proactively deal with tough situations can actually grow and strengthen their relationship over time.

Our culture has veered far away from God's plan for marriage, and many couples have abandoned their dreams of what marriage could be and instead settle for simply hanging on. My hope is you'll apply the principles from this book to create a marriage that is based in God's original design. A relationship meant to *joyfully* last until "death do us part."

In this book you will learn the concept of developing Marital Rules of Engagement. It's a framework to help you proactively consider challenging situations you will encounter. You will learn how to develop jointly agreed upon guidelines (rules) to help you get through them as a couple when they do occur.

This book focuses on key areas of marriage using life-tested philosophies, tips, and techniques to help you proactively create and grow the type of relationship that you really desire. These aren't merely theories, but rather practical processes that can be adopted by any married couple willing to commit to long-term growth and success. I openly share stories from my own life and marriage in the hope that you will benefit from my learning. We can all learn from those that have gone before us.

As you read this book, discuss it with your spouse and complete the exercises at the end of each chapter. Through these discussions, you'll discover some attitudes and behaviors in your relationship that may be counterproductive – shining a light on those is the first step to making change. You will also learn positive new actions that can make your marriage stronger and more enjoyable. It's not hard to be married, but it takes effort to have a *shocking marriage* that positively stands out from our culture.

If you're going through this as a small group study, refer to the Study Guide at the end of the book. There you will find questions and discussion starters that are appropriate in a group setting. My hope is that by studying this with other couples, you will learn that you are not alone in the issues or challenges that you face in your own marriage. That will allow you to encourage one another both now and in the future.

PART 1

REFOCUS YOUR MARRIAGE

CHAPTER 1
DESIRE A SHOCKING MARRIAGE

We live in a culture that puts far more emphasis on weddings than it does on marriage. In 2019, the average cost of a wedding in the United States was just over $33,900[1] and took fourteen months of planning. That's an average! That means that for every simple wedding you've been to, there is at least one extravagant one to offset it. In that same year, only 44 percent of engaged couples entered into any form of premarital counseling[2]. Of those that did, the median time spent in counseling was around eight hours.

Think about it this way. As a culture, we spend fourteen months planning for a single eight-hour day, but

---

1   cnbc.com/2020/02/13/how-much-the-average-wedding-cost-in-2019.html

2   healthresearchfunding.org/20-significant-premarital-counseling-statistics/

only one day planning for a lifetime of marriage! Is it any wonder our divorce rate is so high? Many marriages start off on a high note and slowly erode over time. Once the honeymoon phase is over, comfort sets in. Comfort is soon followed by complacency, then boredom, and finally discontent. It is in this phase where marriages dissolve or continue in a dead and loveless condition.

Marriage has become fodder for humor both on television and in the movies. Couples are routinely seen disparaging one another or sneaking around trying to conceal their activities from their spouses. We find ourselves so deeply immersed in this culture that we have accepted, and sometimes even adopted, these negative attitudes and behaviors The God-ordained sanctity of marriage has degraded over time, and the stigma once associated with divorce has all but vanished.

These negative attitudes and behaviors have become so common we are shocked when we see a long-married couple still truly in love. Be honest. If you see a couple in their forties or older enjoying conversation, flirting, holding hands, or engaging in playful banter, you probably assume they are newlyweds or on their second or third marriage. We're just not used to seeing couples act like that after an extended time together.

A shocking marriage stands apart from these cultural norms. Regardless of the size or cost of the wedding, the early stages of marriage are merely a baseline in terms of happiness and satisfaction. With focus and intentionality, the marriage builds. There are still challenges and tough seasons, but like fine wine, a shocking marriage gets better with time.

This book is targeted at couples who are ready to commit to a better marriage; a shocking marriage. That does not imply your marriage is currently in trouble, nor does it insinuate your relationship is mediocre. It's simply recognizing no matter where you are in your relationship, there's room for improvement. If you're in a good marriage, think in terms of great. If you're in a great marriage, work toward making it extraordinary. If you're engaged to be married—perfect! No better time to plan for a promising future than now. Don't settle for a marriage that is just okay. Dream big about what your marriage could and should be.

Focus and Intentionality

Shocking marriages don't just happen. The first step to creating a shocking marriage is focus and intentionality. Making a conscious effort to prioritize your spouse and their needs will set you apart from the average couple. It doesn't mean ignoring other key people in your life. It just means not taking your spouse for granted and assuming you can tend to them later.

A friend told me about her dad's experience in coaching a girl's middle school softball team. He agreed to do this as a favor to his daughter, and he saw it as an opportunity to spend time with his two granddaughters. His experience was less than ideal. The team resided in an affluent area, and many of the girls were also on other, sometimes more prestigious, softball teams. He never knew how many kids would actually show up for practice or even for a given game. There were a few times when they didn't have enough players to compete. This team was not a top priority for many of these girls, so they came when they could but missed out otherwise—often without even bothering to notify the coach. Membership on this team meant little to these girls and was just another item on their overcommitted schedules. They had virtually no chance of success.

Too many marriages in our culture resemble the dynamics of this team. Spouses become just another person who needs attention. Sadly, because they are taken for granted, they fall to the bottom of the priority list behind kids' needs, career needs, social needs, church needs, and other distractions. It's no wonder that over time, these marriages dissolve. Just like the softball team, they have no chance of winning.

You may no longer be a newlywed. In fact, you may have been married for years or even decades by now. You may be on your marriage or even third third marriage. You may assume that you are simply stuck with the relationship you are in. It is important to note that *where you have been is of far less importance than where you are headed.* God does not want you to be in a mediocre marriage, now or ever. He wants you to be blessed abundantly in your relationship. If you want to pursue and achieve a shocking marriage, there's no better time to start than the present.

In 2013, contemporary Christian artist Casting Crowns launched a song called *Thrive*.[3] I love the chorus. It includes the following:

> We know we were made for so much more
> Than ordinary lives
> It's time for us to more than just survive
> We were made to thrive

I can't think of a better descriptor for a shocking marriage. As you read through this book, I want to challenge you to consider areas of your marriage where you may be just surviving. Be honest with yourself. These areas may

---

not look any worse to you than what you see in most other marriages around you. But that's not what we're shooting for. We're looking for excellence in marriage. We're looking to thrive. We want the world to look at our marriages and find them shocking.

What does a shocking marriage look like? I liken this to the way Supreme Court Justice Potter Stewart described his threshold test for obscenity in 1964: "I know it when I see it." Let me give you examples of shocking marriages in couples that I've seen personally:

- The elderly couple that hold hands while sitting in church every week.
- The couple married for thirty-plus years that playfully flirt together in the checkout line at the grocery.
- The couple that prioritize date nights and leave their kids home with a sitter.
- The middle-aged couple in a cooking class together for the first time.
- The couple that speaks highly of each other when alone with their friends.
- The spouse that avoids correcting or criticizing their partner as they recount a story to friends.
- The couple that has a "secret rendezvous" midweek during lunch.

It's not that any one of these activities is shocking but, rather, the intentionality that lies behind them. Couples that do these things work at marriage and are always striving for a better relationship. They don't take each other for granted. They give their partners high priority as they go through life. They avoid complacency. They understand their spouse is a gift from God and should be honored accordingly.

Casting a Vision

I've heard it said, "You can't out achieve your dreams." If you have never considered a relationship that is better than where you are today, that's as good as your marriage will ever be. You may have had dreams early on of what marriage could be, but over time you have come to settle for far less. You don't give it much thought, you assume things are fine, and you've quit trying. If that is you, here is my advice. **STOP IT!** God does not intend for you to be in an average marriage. He wants it to be the greatest experience you can have with another person. It's time to dream bigger, so you can achieve more. Envisioning your desired future is the first step in the process.

Over the course of my professional career, I've launched several new project teams, organizations, and even businesses. Some were overwhelming successes, and others, quite frankly, were outright failures. In every case, the difference between success and failure was the quality of the vision at the outset. Those efforts with a bold, solid vision were far more successful than those where I attempted to direct the future as I went along.

In business, a vision should be lofty and cause an organization to stretch in order to achieve it. Amazon didn't strive to be just a seller of books. Their vision statement is "to be Earth's most customer-centric company, where customers can find and discover anything they might want to buy online." Twitter didn't dream of becoming another texting replacement app. Their vision is "to give everyone the power to create and share ideas and information instantly, without barriers." These companies have bold visions to be the biggest and the best at what they do.

A solid vision for marriage should be something that causes both spouses to look to the future, inspiring them to stretch and work together to achieve something meaningful. When revisited over time, a couple can not only check their progress, but make necessary adjustments ensuring they are headed in the right direction.

No engaged couple dreams about entering into a dull, routine relationship that both partners find merely tolerable. Rather, they dream of spending a lifetime of undiminishing love, raising a family, and growing old together. These things are fine, but by themselves do not create a vision. Relationships change over time, hopefully for the better but, unfortunately, sometimes it's for the worse. No couple married for ten years will claim that their feelings for each other haven't changed over time. The honeymoon phase fades away for everyone. Without ongoing and intentional effort, the simplistic dream once shared by the couple will slowly evaporate.

Working toward a shared vision will keep the marriage on track and growing in a positive direction. Ask yourself: What do I want my marriage to look like five years from now and beyond? What will we have to do to create a shocking marriage?

Elements of a Vision

If you've ever worked in a corporate or a nonprofit setting you may have participated in a meeting where you worked on creating a vision statement. Oftentimes these are long tedious meetings that devolve into endless wordsmithing. Memories of this experience may scare you away from exerting such an effort for your marriage. Don't make it that hard; just capture some thoughts or goals that you can both agree to work toward. You're not carving anything permanently into stone. These can and should be revisited and revised as needed over time. In fact, that would be a very positive activity to do as a couple every few years.

Here are some elements that are included in the marriage vision I created with my wife, Tara.

- We want our marriage to honor Christ in all that we say and do.
- We want to raise a healthy and happy family but keep the spousal relationship a top priority.
- We want to *love being married* to each other and will take efforts to make that so.
- Fun is a top priority for both of us.
- We will assess our relationship periodically and focus on areas where we can make improvements.

A marital vision is not a day-to-day set of rules that must be followed. It is a compass to keep you headed in the right general direction. Refer back to your vision from time to time to see how you are doing. In our case, we may discover that it's been a while since we have had fun together. Knowing that is a top priority will inspire us to plan something we both enjoy. If we didn't have it documented, we might forget that is important to us as a couple. The key is to recognize when you start to go off course and make the necessary adjustments to get back on track.

Use the questions at the end of the chapter to help capture your thoughts. Write them down and create a starting point. Your vision can and should be revisited over time and will be perfected as you grow together as a couple.

Remarriage

Maybe-this is not your first marriage. You've been married and divorced and find yourself either preparing for or in another marriage now. Like others in your same situation, you bring battle scars into your current relationship. Even though your past marriage failed, that does not mean you as an individual are a failure. God has a plan for you and your life that includes your current spouse.

The people I know who are on their second (or third or even fourth) marriage seem to fall into one of two camps. The first group wants to blot their previous marriage(s) from their memory. They see it as an awful experience and choose to never spend time thinking about it. The last thing they want is to discuss that relationship with their new spouse. While it may seem like a way to avoid stress, that attitude does nothing to change behaviors. In time, old habits and behaviors return and create the same problems encountered before. As a result, they find themselves once again in an unhappy, unhealthy marriage, and threat of another divorce hangs over their heads.

The second camp is very different. These people also went through a failed marriage, but instead of ignoring their past, they spend time analyzing it. Instead of trying to place blame, they look at their own attitudes and behaviors and determine what they could/should have done differently. They talk openly with their new spouse about these issues and ask to be held accountable to the changes they desire to make. They typically make a commitment to one another that they never want to go through another divorce and agree they are both in the relationship for the long haul. They have learned from the past and commit to working together toward a better future.

I have seen that those who openly consider their past and choose to learn from it tend to be in much more satisfying relationships than those who attempt to block it from their memory or refuse to take a critical look at what actually went wrong. Learn from the Spanish philosopher George Santayana: "Those who do not learn history are doomed to repeat it." Don't fall into the same patterns and traps that you did the first time around.

Follow God's Design for Marriage

Marriage is an institution that God arranged near the beginning of creation. He determined that one man would enter into a covenant relationship with one woman. The two would become one flesh and be together for the rest of their natural lives.

In the New Testament book of Ephesians, we see that God provides couples with instructions through the apostle Paul for living as a married couple. These verses apply as much today as they did when they were written nearly 2000 years ago.

Before he gets into specific instructions for the husband and wife, he writes the following:

> Do not get drunk on wine, which leads to debauchery. Instead, be filled with the Spirit, speaking to one another with psalms, hymns, and songs from the Spirit. Sing and make music from your heart to the Lord, always giving thanks to God the Father for everything, in the name of our Lord Jesus Christ.
>
> Ephesians 5:18-20 NIV

Paul realizes that getting through the day can be tough sometimes. That can involve many aspects of our lives, but it certainly includes marriage. He points out that alcohol is not the solution. Instead, he points out the need for us to be filled with the Holy Spirit. He realizes that in our selfish nature, it will be impossible for us to look beyond ourselves and our own needs to focus on our spouse. But with God's help, in the form of the Holy Spirit, we can do just that. We can view our spouse as of primary importance and put their needs before our own.

Once we have the power of the Spirit working within us, he goes on to give specific instructions on living as a married couple. The first bit of instruction he provides is to both the husband and the wife.

> Submit to one another out of reverence for Christ.
>
> Ephesians 5:21 NIV

We see here that both husbands and wives are to submit to one another, focusing on each other's needs. This is a critical first step, as it sets the very tone of the marriage. Neither partner is dominating, nor are they living independently. They are aligned in their thinking and in their mutual submission.

From here, Paul goes on to first give specific instruction to the wife, then to the husband.

> Wives, submit yourselves to your own husbands as you do to the Lord. For the husband is the head of the wife as Christ is the head of the church, his body, of which he is the Savior. Now as the church submits to Christ, so also wives should submit to their husbands in everything.
>
> Ephesians 5:22-24 NIV

Here we see further instruction for wives. It is important to note that this verse does not contradict the previous verse that dealt with mutual submission. This verse does not deal with meeting each other's needs, but rather begins to establish structure in the marriage relationship.

This verse is often misused and misunderstood. Many women tend to hate it, thinking that it puts them in a subordinate role to their husband. Many men have misused this verse to control their wives. Let's clarify this passage to illustrate how when used appropriately, it can help to build a Shocking Marriage.

1. **Submission (mentioned here) is about structure, not control.** God views marriage strategically and has recommended a structure in which it can best thrive. Without structure, chaos reigns. This is true in companies, governments, social clubs and marriage. If couples are truly focused on mutual submission (meeting each other's needs) this then implies the role of final decision maker for the marriage itself. Submitting in this manner is not showing weakness, it's simply agreeing to the structure set forth by God.

2. **Submit to the position, not the person.** Wives are told to submit to their own husbands. Not because they are men, but because they hold the position of husband. We read in the book of Galatians that there is no male or female – we're all equal before Christ. There may be a situation where the husband works for the wife in a business or at a company. In that situation, he would be called to submit to her position. But in marital

situations, she is called to submit to his position of husband.

3. **Submission is about responsibility, not authority.** Nowhere in the Bible does it say that a husband has any authority over his wife, nor does it tell the husband to command his wife to submit. Submission is completely voluntary on the part of the wife.

Another part of this verse that is often misunderstood or mis-applied is in verse 23 where it says the husband is the head of the wife... The original Greek word for head is kephale. Like many words, it has a range of meanings, but it is not the word that is used for authority. A more likely translation would be like headwaters or source. The husband is the head of his wife, as in the one who can lift her up, edify her, and help her grow. He is not her authority, Christ is her authority.

Paul goes on in the following verses to provide specific instruction for husbands.

Husbands, love your wives, just as Christ loved the church and gave himself up for her to make her holy, cleansing her by the washing with water through the word, and to present her to himself as a radiant church, without stain or wrinkle or any other blemish, but holy and blameless. In this same way, husbands ought to love their wives as their own bodies. He who loves his wife loves himself. After all, no one ever hated their own body, but they feed and care for their body, just as Christ does the church— for we are members of his body. "For this reason, a man will leave his father and mother and be united to his wife, and the two will become one flesh." This is a profound mystery—but I am talking about Christ and the church. However, each one of you also must love his wife as he loves himself, and the wife must respect her husband.

Ephesians 5:25-33 NIV

Christ gave Himself for the church intentionally and purposefully. That's how husbands are called to love their wives. God wants you to have a shocking marriage and has provided the structure to enable you to experience one. He has given you His Spirit to coach you along the way. Don't try to do this on your own strength and power. Use the roadmap and the tools He has provided to move you forward to the marriage of which you dreamed!

Summary

God designed marriage and intends for it to be the most incredible relationship we can have with another person. If you do this God's way, your relationship will look different from a typical marriage in our culture – and that's a good thing! It takes focus and intentionality to create a Shocking Marriage, but it is worth it. Creating a vision for where you want to go as a couple and how you want to interact is important. You put time and effort into the things that are most important to you in life. Marriage should be near the top of your list.

Discussion Questions

What are the vision elements that you would like to strive for from this day forward? It all starts with a conversation. Work through the following questions with your spouse:

- Independently list five words you would use to describe your ideal marriage relationship (e.g., fun, passionate, stable, comfortable, etc.). Once you have each listed your words, share your list with your spouse. What words do you have in common? What words are different? Are you surprised at any of their words? Discuss this as a couple.
- What long-term marital goals (vision elements) do you and your spouse share?
- How well is your current relationship heading toward those goals? What needs to change if a course correction is in order?
- Are you using God's help in your marriage or striving to do things in your own power?
- Think of couples who you believe have shocking marriages. What are the specific things about them that make you think that? What specific things have you seen them do to indicate that they give each other priority?
- What is one "shocking" behavior you can incorporate into your marriage in the next week? The next month? The next year?

CHAPTER 2

BUILD A SOLID FOUNDATION

In an ideal world, marriage would start off well and improve over time. It would appreciate like a valuable asset, getting better and better as the years pass. Unfortunately, it doesn't always happen that way. Some marriages start off in a dysfunctional state and erode almost immediately. Others start off fine but slowly degrade due to lack of attention. No matter where your marriage is today, you can make it better.

If you're a homeowner, consider your house. It requires maintenance and upkeep over time. You can focus solely on the more visible parts of the home like landscaping, paint and décor, but that won't keep the structure from deteriorating. Your home is built on a foundation. As long as the foundation remains solid, the house will stand through most storms. But if through neglect, the foundation begins to crumble, it doesn't take long for the entire house to collapse.

Jesus taught on this concept in the following passage.

Anyone who listens to my teaching and follows it is wise, like a person who builds a house on solid rock. Though the rain comes in torrents and the floodwaters rise and the winds beat against that house, it won't collapse because it is built on bedrock. But anyone who hears my teaching and doesn't obey it is foolish, like a person who builds a house on sand. When the rains and floods come and the winds beat against that house, it will collapse with a mighty crash.

Matthew 7:24–27 NLT

Marriage is a beautiful and tangible application of this teaching. Marriages built on the rock of Jesus will weather the inevitable storms that come in life. Those built only on passion or feelings are like the house built on sand. Living on the beach sounds great at the outset. Who doesn't want a life filled with white sand, crystal-blue water, and palm trees? But living in a cabana isn't so appealing in a hurricane. When the wind and rain of hardship starts to tear at the structure of your marriage and there is nowhere to go for refuge from the storm, the beach loses its luster. If you don't create a foundation built on rock, your marriage may not survive. Marital collapse doesn't happen all at once. Just like a house, a relationship built on a shaky foundation degrades over time. You may attempt repairs, but without shoring up the foundation, these fixes will be mainly cosmetic and short-lived.

We all know couples whose relationship is built on sand. At first, they seem to have it all together in terms of family and careers. But as time goes on, we begin to notice the cracks and missing shingles that exist within their marriage. They attempt to conceal the most visible issues for a while, but at some point, they decide that the effort required to rebuild the relationship is just too great. At that point, they cut their losses and walk away from the whole thing.

Contrast this with the couple that builds their marriage on a solid foundation. The trials these couples face marriage may be no different in terms of frequency or severity, but because of their sure foundation, they are able to weather the storms that come in life. They know the value of proactively maintaining and repairing their relationship, which allows their marriage to appreciate over time.

Our Story – From Sand to Rock

My wife, Tara, and I got married at a young age. I was twenty-one and she was a few months short of her twenty-first birthday. We began dating in high school and continued doing so into college. Like many young couples, we were passionately in love and didn't want to put off being together. Due to our conservative upbringing, neither of us considered it okay to move in together out of wedlock. We got married before my senior year (her junior year) and moved into married student housing at Purdue University. At that age, creating a vision or building a foundation on rock was the last thing on our mind. We just wanted to be together, get through school, find employment, and ultimately transition to our "adult lives."

With no meaningful premarital counseling, we jumped into marriage without much of a plan, let alone a vision. Selfishly, our focus was on what was best for each us as individuals. I went to my classes; she went to hers. We gave no attention to our future. We simply assumed we would figure life out as it came.

The first ten months of marriage went by smoothly and quickly. Being in the honeymoon phase of marriage, conflict was rare and short-lived. Our frustrations were little different from our nonmarried friends, mostly centered on school assignments and class projects. The first real test in our relationship occurred as my senior year came to a close. Though I had an engineering degree from a great school, I graduated in the midst of a nasty recession. I went to every interview on campus and applied to as many openings by mail as I possibly could but got job offers from none of them.

Graduation was exciting, but the feeling of accomplishment was short-lived. The lease on our campus apartment expired within days of the ceremony. With no job in hand and no home to live in, we found ourselves as a newlywed couple moving into my parent's home.

I was blessed with great parents but moving back with them as a young married man was humiliating. I'll never forget the look in Tara's eyes as we moved our few possessions into their home. It's as if she was asking, "What have you gotten me into?" She had a full year left before graduation, didn't know what her future would hold, and wondered if she would even be able to finish college. Adding insult to injury, she was moving in to live with her in-laws. I felt both helpless and useless. I had a wife whom I could neither support nor begin a serious adult life with. There were several quiet days spent worrying and wondering.

Time passed at a snail's pace, but after a couple of weeks, I got a call from one of the companies that I had applied to by mail while still on campus—Whirlpool Corporation. They had an opening for an entry-level industrial engineer at their washing machine factory in Clyde, Ohio. Though I'd never heard of Clyde Ohio I jumped at the opportunity and within days found myself driving the five hours for an interview. Things went well, and within a couple more weeks (of incredibly anxious waiting), I got a job offer. Shortly thereafter, we found ourselves moving to our own place to finally begin our adult, married life.

Things got exciting again. I threw myself into work, and Tara began taking classes at the University of Toledo. New beginnings, independence, and adulthood were now underway. The very things that we had been waiting for now became the primary focus of our lives. We had new friendships, personal endeavors and work/class schedules to fill our time, but we began to take our relationship with each other for granted. Without realizing it, we were building our marriage on sand, and we saw no reason to do anything differently.

Our life in Ohio continued on. The honeymoon phase of marriage was wearing off, but things were still okay. We found ourselves assimilating into our new community. I was an engineer at a huge factory in a small town, and Tara drove an hour to and from class each day. Being new in my job, I wanted to fit in and establish relationships. Most of my coworkers were native to the area, and many of them had worked their way up from the factory floor. I don't know if it was unique to this particular small town or simply the culture of factory life, but I found myself being exposed to influences and values that were foreign to me. As an example, most people I worked with were married, but many saw no real problem with "fooling around on the side." Gossip was rampant in terms of who was sleeping with whom.

A typical Friday afternoon would include a trip to the bar across the street for happy hour, where many of my coworkers would stay until the wee hours the following morning. As this was contrary to how I'd been raised, I was surprised by their attitudes and behaviors. I remember asking one respected guy in our department, "How does your wife put up with you staying out all hours and carousing with women?" His response was simply, "She's got five kids, where's she going to go?" While his answer repulsed me, he was an ongoing, unhealthy influence that I worked with every day. Though I didn't agree with many of the attitudes around me, my immersion in this culture began to affect me. The language I picked up and the lack of respect I began showing Tara all began to increase. Since everyone else went to happy hour on Friday, I found myself going as well. At first, it was just a drop-in visit, but over time, I found myself staying far longer than I'd promised Tara. When I did get home, I was typically not in a state of mind to be focused on her needs. She began to resent my lack of respect, my drinking and my absence from home.

In an effort to establish relationships outside of work, we got involved with various community-based organizations (in hindsight, it seemed like everything except church!) where we met a variety of people and made new friends. One night we went out with two other couples. One of the couples was each on their second marriage. We had just finished dinner at their home when they began to argue about something that (apparently) had occurred earlier in the day. While this was uncomfortable for the other four of us, it was a situation we had witnessed in the past. The argument escalated quickly, and before we knew it, the wife was storming out of the room screaming at her husband, "I should just divorce you. I left my first husband for far less." In hindsight, I'm not sure if we were more shocked by the magnitude of her threat or by the casual manner in which her husband dismissed it, as if it were nothing. While he was somewhat embarrassed this happened in front of us, his response was simply to smile and wave his hand. "She'll get over it."

When Tara and I got home that night, we were both shaken by what we'd experienced. We sat silently on the couch for quite a while. The evening's events forced us to contemplate our own marriage. Finally, with a tear in my eye, I looked at Tara and asked her, "You'd never threaten me with divorce, would you?" It took her much longer to respond than I would have hoped. The conversation that ensued cut me to the core. I didn't realize how much my acquired selfish behavior had affected and even injured her. At some level, she had begun to question our future together, deeply concerned at the negative direction we were heading. While I was seemingly oblivious, she had begun to see our "house" for what it was—a degrading structure with no solid foundation.

As our conversation continued, I apologized for my behaviors and told her that I never wanted to consider divorce. She responded that was not her desire, either, but went on to say that things needed to change for that to be off the table. Once I was aware of the issues with our relationship, I could no longer ignore them. Being an engineer by training, I began to work on the problems that had surfaced one by one. It was exhausting, but I put in the effort, and Tara could see I was trying. After a couple of weeks, I nervously approached her and said, "I never want to get a divorce. I promise I will stay with you forever if you'll have me." Her response back was the most comforting I'd ever heard. "I agree. I'll never threaten divorce or leave you either." It was during that period that we came to realize that our relationship was not as stable as we had perceived it to be. We didn't yet know what it meant to build our marriage on the rock of Jesus, but we knew that we did not want to remain in the condition we were in. It was time to move forward.

Soon after this, I was promoted to a new job in Michigan. Tara and I both saw this as a chance for a new beginning where we could start building our marriage in a more positive manner. Our first child was turning three, and I felt strongly that we needed to find and start going to a church somewhere. I had gone to church every Sunday as a kid, and I was determined that my children would do the same. While Sunday mornings were never my favorite time growing up, I still figured it was the right thing to do for them.

Our goal was to find a church that would be comfortable for both of us and have a great kid's program. By comfortable, I mean a place where we could attend on Sundays but not be expected to do much else. A place where we could make good friends, but not ones who were too pious or judgmental. If we could walk away after service feeling good about ourselves and inspired to be better people in the upcoming week, that would be a plus.

We tried out several different denominational churches that we had heard of before but found none to our liking. After several months of searching we visited an Evangelical Free Church near our home. While we had never heard of this type of church, in our minds it sounded perfect. In the age of sugar-free, caffeine-free, and fat-free, we assumed this would be a church that was free of evangelism. The last thing we wanted was to be challenged in our faith or pushed to recruit other people to join the church.

It turns out we were wrong. Quite wrong. This was a Bible-believing church that had a tremendous focus on outreach. Our first Sunday there found me squirming in my seat as the sermon convicted me of my lifestyle and made me aware there was something (someone) missing. In spite of my discomfort, the people there were warm and loving, and we felt ourselves drawn back in the following weeks. Within a few months of attending, we both accepted Jesus into our lives as our Lord and Savior. God began directing us individually and reshaping us as a couple. It became clear that we needed to build our marriage on a new foundation. That has remained our focus ever since.

Refocusing our marriage was the greatest single thing we ever did. We went from considering only our own needs to putting each other first. That didn't solve all of our problems, as you will read in the coming chapters, we certainly weathered many storms after that point. But our solid foundation has kept our marriage standing through all of them.

The Trinity's Role in Marriage

The theology of the Trinity is foundational to the Christian faith. It also applies directly to marriage. While the details of the Trinity may be confusing, the basic idea is that God exists in three parts: God the Father, Jesus the Son, and the Holy Spirit who is God's presence living inside of us. That's one God. Three in one. As you will see in the following, each aspect of God has a role in our ongoing lives and our marriages.

God the Architect

We see in the very first verses of the Bible (Genesis 1) that God created everything, including the sun, the planets, earth, water, animals, people, even life at a microscopic level with complexity beyond our comprehension. We also learn from scripture that God is all-knowing (omniscient), all-powerful (omnipotent), and everywhere at every time (omnipresent). This clearly puts God in the role of Master Designer or Universal Architect, the ultimate creator and designer of life as we know it.

As with other aspects of His master design, marriage originated with God and is mentioned in the second chapter of the first book of the Bible (Genesis 2). God declared that it was not good for man to live alone, so He created a helpmate for Adam. In verse 25, we see that Eve is referred to as Adam's wife. They became one flesh and were intended to stay together for eternity. But as the story continues, sin entered the world, and the first couple was exiled from paradise. All forms of trouble and distress entered the world including, we can assume, problems in marriage.

As fallen people, our culture has veered far away from God's original plan. This is not a recent phenomenon. We see early examples in the Old Testament of infidelity and polygamy. King David so lusted after the beautiful Bathsheba that he had her husband assigned to the front lines of battle, knowing he would be killed. His son, Solomon, the wisest human who ever lived, had eight hundred wives and over two hundred concubines! All of his earthly wisdom could not ultimately overcome the influence these women had over him. As time went on, Solomon began building temples to the various gods that his wives worshipped, and he ultimately fell out of favor with God.

> History merely repeats itself. It has all been done before. Nothing under the sun is truly new. Sometimes people say, "Here is something new!" But actually it is old; nothing is ever truly new. We don't remember what happened in the past,

and in future generations, no one will remember what we are doing now.

Ecclesiastes 1:9-11 NLT

Just as this scripture indicates, thousands of years after this was written (by Solomon himself), many couples abandon God's plan and decide to do things their own way. They look at the architect of the universe and everything in it and say, "I understand your intention, but I think I know a better way . . ." The results speak for themselves. Marriage is destined to work better when we build our relationship according to the Master Architect's design.

Jesus the Foundation

As we saw in Matthew, building your foundation on rock happens by hearing Jesus's words and following His teaching. Jesus is the foundation on which we should build our marriages. But what does that mean? What does that look like? Before you can build your marriage on Jesus as your foundation, you must first have a *personal* relationship with Him. You have to see your need for Him.

For everyone has sinned; we all fall short of God's glorious standard. Yet God, in his grace, freely makes us right in his sight. He did this through Christ Jesus when he freed us from the penalty for our sins.

Romans 3:23-24 NLT

There's nothing you can do on your own power that will make you worthy of being with God. No amount of community service, good works, spirituality, or church attendance will earn you eternal life. But God didn't leave you in a hopeless state.

For God so loved the world that He gave His one and only Son, that whoever believes in Him shall not perish, but have eternal life.

John 3:16 NIV

Salvation is a free gift offered to everyone. All you have to do is admit you can't get there on your own and accept the gift that is provided through Jesus. As believers, we cherish grace and view it as the most remarkable gift that could possibly be received.

If you and your spouse have accepted Christ, that's a great starting point. Now you need to agree to make Him the foundation of your marriage. Jesus should be the primary relationship for each of you as individuals. After Him, your relationship with each other comes second. If you get this out of order, your foundation is not solid, and your marriage will suffer. You cannot put your faith on a back burner and expect to receive God's blessings, assistance, or direction. Make Jesus the focal point of your entire relationship.

As humans, we are naturally wired to desire justice. Justice is defined loosely as getting something that is deserved. Right should be rewarded and wrong punished. Fortunately for us, scripture shows we are not limited to receiving only that which we deserve. Jesus died on the cross that we might be forgiven for the wrongs we have done—past, present, and future. It is only through

His sacrifice that we can be seen as blameless and considered worthy of eternal life.

That is where grace comes into play. Grace is defined as the undeserved favor of God for those who are otherwise under condemnation. If we truly got what we deserved, none of us would be worthy to enter heaven to spend eternity with God.

Just as we are freely given grace from God, we are called to extend grace to others. That holds especially true for our spouses. How do we do this? We do this when we incorporate kind words and encouragement into our language. We do this when we don't condemn or attack our spouse. We do this when we forgive. We do this when we don't hold on to past issues. And we do this when we show love even when we're not especially feeling it. It is not reasonable to be able to show grace if you've not first experienced it. Understanding and accepting God's grace is a critical first step to putting Him first in your marriage.

Holy Spirit — the Source of Power and Security

So you've committed to God's design for your marriage, and you've decided to build your foundation on your collective faith in Jesus. What else is needed? Homes work better when they are connected to a power source. Electricity, natural gas, and even Internet are no longer considered luxuries, but rather basic needs. You might be able to survive in a home without these things, but life is certainly easier when they are provided.

I have a Nest thermostat in my home. It is a smart home device that learns my preferences and behaviors over time and adjusts the temperature accordingly. It knows when we're home and when we're away. While we used to constantly be tweaking our old thermostat, we now always feel comfortable in our home while at the same time saving money by not overheating or cooling an empty house. As a result, I have ceded control over to this device. It has learned my preferences and my dislikes. I now trust it knows best and always has me in an optimum environment.

I have a friend who got an identical Nest thermostat as a present. It's been several months, but he has not gotten around to installing it yet. It sits in a box on his counter. We both own the same product. His Nest has as much capability as mine does, but he has chosen not to enjoy any of the benefits that it offers. I've talked to him about how easy it is to use; in fact, I've even offered to install it for him. He likes to be in control and doesn't like the thought of this smart device running his environment for him.

Marriages are no different. You can have a well-designed relationship built on a foundation of faith, but it will require a tremendous amount of effort on your part if you try to sustain it without wisdom and power from the Holy Spirit.

> But the Advocate, the Holy Spirit, whom the Father will send in my name, will teach you all things and will remind you of everything I have said to you.
>
> John 14:26 NIV

In this verse, Jesus promised the Spirit to all who believe. While all believers have access to the Holy Spirit, many choose not to engage with Him. As Christ's followers, all we have to do is open up and begin to consciously interact with the Spirit in our lives. He's available, powerful and desires to have a relationship with each one of us. When we allow the Spirit to power our lives and our marriages, life becomes much simpler.

> But the Holy Spirit produces this kind of fruit in our lives: love, joy, peace, patience, kindness, goodness, faithfulness, gentleness, and self-control.
>
> Galatians 5:22–23 NLT

What marriage wouldn't be better if it exhibited these characteristics? This fruit is not something that you consciously strive for, but rather a natural outcome of living under the direction of the Holy Spirit.

In a "smart marriage," the Holy Spirit provides more than power. He also provides protection and security for those who choose to be connected. Just as you might have smoke alarms and carbon monoxide detectors in your home to warn you of unseen dangers, the Spirit can do the same for you in your marriage. Every marriage will have natural seasons of highs and lows. During low seasons, negative thoughts may creep into your mind regarding your spouse. Hints of dissatisfaction, mistrust, or even unjustified anger could be examples. It's at these times that you need to seek the guidance of the Holy Spirit to check the source of these thoughts. Remember, there are forces that don't want believers to be in happy marriages.

> For we are not fighting against flesh-and-blood enemies, but against evil rulers and authorities of the unseen world, against mighty powers in this dark world, and against evil spirits in the heavenly places.
>
> Ephesians 6:12 NLT

The Spirit will help you to recognize these thoughts for what they are—destructive input intended to cause discontent in a relationship. Once you discern this, you can literally pray them away.

God wants us to have blessed marriages that bring Him glory. It grieves Him when He sees married believers sin against each other through conflict, separation, and divorce. And it certainly damages the credibility of the church when our marriages are no different from those in our culture. But we can't have the marriage that God intends for us to have if we don't make Him the center of it. When we try to bolster and protect our marriages with our own efforts, we're no different than the world around us.

It takes determination and discipline to create and maintain a great marriage. Unfortunately, this kind of self-discipline does not come easily. This is not a new condition, nor is it tied directly to our current culture. Nearly two thousand years ago, the apostle Paul wrote about this very issue.

> I don't really understand myself, for I want to do what is right, but I don't do it. Instead, I do what I hate
>
> Romans 7:15 NLT)

He elaborates a couple of verses later,

> And I know that nothing good lives in me, that is, in my sinful nature. I want to do what is right, but I can't. I want to do what is good, but I don't. I don't want to do what is wrong, but I do it anyway.
>
> Romans 7:18–20

I am sure marriage counselors around the world have heard these same sentiments. God Himself first envisioned marriage and didn't intend for us to enter into such a complex relationship without Him. If we rely solely on our own strength, we will most certainly fall short of His expectations, as well as our own. The good news is, as believers, we can partner with God in our marriages. The following verses, heard often in wedding ceremonies, provide a great picture for what this should look like.

Two people are better off than one, for they can help each other succeed. If one person falls, the other can reach out and help. But someone who falls alone is in real trouble. Likewise, two people lying close together can keep each other warm. But how can one be warm alone? A person standing alone can be attacked and defeated, but two can stand back-to-back and conquer. Three are even better, for a triple-braided cord is not easily broken.

Ecclesiastes 4:9–12 NLT

You and your spouse are more capable and powerful together than either of you could possibly be on your own, especially when you are committed to the same vision and goals for your marriage. Add the Holy Spirit as the third strand, and your cord (relationship) is not easily broken. It's ultimately about being Spirit-disciplined, not self-disciplined.

Summary

Creating a Shocking Marriage is not something you can do on your own power. Fortunately, you don't have to. Using the tools and power that God provides will enable you to create the type of marriage that He intends you to enjoy. Build your relationship on the foundation of Christ, and use the Holy Spirit to empower you through the course of your marriage.

Discussion Questions

- What does the author mean when he talks about building a marriage on rock instead of sand?
- What would you say that your marriage is currently built on?
- Are there ways you could shore up your marital foundation?
- Using the house analogy, what areas of your marriage should you focus on maintaining? What areas, if any, need immediate repair?
- Have you prioritized Jesus as being *first* in your marriage? What does that look like?
- Are you utilizing the power the Holy Spirit provides in your relationship, or are you doing things on your own strength? How could you begin to plug in to the power that God has provided for you?

PART 2
PROTECT YOUR MARRIAGE

CHAPTER 3
RULES OF ENGAGEMENT - FRAMEWORK

I know a guy who manages his investment portfolio on a near daily basis. He wants to see what stocks are overperforming and which are falling short. He has a series of formulas and guidelines that he uses to direct his buying and selling. Based on his findings, he makes continuous adjustments in an effort to maximize his return. He once gave me this investment advice: "You've got to keep a constant eye on your portfolio, or it will get away from you. It's critical to spot trends—see how the market is reacting to various stimuli. By making little adjustments on a regular basis, you can avoid any huge surprises." To this day, he takes tremendous pride in his savvy investment strategy.

On a side note, he's divorced now. It's not because he spent so much time managing his money, but rather he spent too little time watching his marriage. He hadn't noticed that his wife had been unhappy. She craved attention and affection from him that she wasn't receiving. Over time, she grew further and further from him emotionally. Eventually, she was lured away by the attention of another man who was willing to satisfy her needs. That he noticed!

When his wife left him, he was shocked and felt completely betrayed. He was unwilling to grasp the role he had played in the failure of his marriage. He didn't realize had he spent a fraction of the attention on his wife that he did on his finances, he could have seen trends coming, established some guidelines, and made adjustments. He may have been able to save his marriage. As it turned out, the return on his marriage investment bombed.

The Rules of Engagement framework allows you to create rules for your marriage that both you and your spouse agree to. The intent is to have safeguards in place so that when you are faced with a given situation, you know how to proceed. In addition, rules can help to keep you on track toward your vision. There is no way that you could anticipate or plan for any possible trial that you might face. You will find the discipline of having some effective rules in place can help you no matter the situation.

Creating our Rules

Once Tara and I determined we would build our future relationship on rock instead of sand, we realized we would need to do things differently moving forward. We decided to focus on two different areas. First, we would intentionally take the time to periodically do a self-assessment on our relationship. The reason for this was we never wanted to be surprised again as to how the other was feeling about our relationship. We knew it was better to understand an issue early than to let it fester unchecked over time. This simply consisted of having a reflective conversation. How have things been going? What's gone well? Where have we struggled? Where are we headed? The goal was to ensure neither of us was assuming how the other was feeling in terms of the marriage. Knowing we always go out for a nice dinner on our anniversary, we agreed that could be a great time to have this discussion. Having it on a set and memorable day has kept us from procrastinating or forgetting about it all together!

Having the annual assessment was a great first step, but we realized we had a need to improve things on an ongoing basis as well. One of the areas where we struggled as a couple surrounded conflict, mainly because our individual styles of fighting were radically different. Our arguments, though infrequent, caused so much frustration for each of us that we knew we needed to do something different. Never disagreeing again was unrealistic, so in a time of peace and calm, we created some guidelines on which we could both agree. Our goal was to ensure conflict would ultimately move our relationship forward and not cause lasting damage. That discussion created the foundation of something we came to call our marital rules of engagement (ROE). The Cambridge Dictionary defines "rules of engagements" (ROE) as: "orders that soldiers fighting in a war are given about what they can and cannot do.[4]" It's not that we saw ourselves as combatants in our marriage, but we liked the parallel.

---

4   https://dictionary.cambridge.org/us/dictionary/english/rules-of-engagement

Implementing rules of engagement surrounding conflict improved our relationship immediately and dramatically. Once a spat was over, it was over. No more walking around the house not speaking. No more cold shoulders in bed, and no more fear of starting the argument over by saying the wrong thing.

As a part of this process, we took some time to figure out if there was a typical cause for our conflict. We came to the realization most of the time, it was a misalignment of our expectations. In other words, when faced with a new situation I would assume one path forward, and Tara would assume another. We were both guilty of assuming the other was in agreement, so we never took the time to hear each other's perspectives before devising a plan. This was a true "A-Ha" moment for us. We had found a way to minimize the impact of our arguments, but could this same concept work to avoid or reduce future ones?

Our marital rules of engagement worked so effectively in terms of conflict, we wondered if we could apply this concept to other areas of our relationship. Sure, fighting fair is critical, but how many other areas would benefit from having preestablished guidelines? What about intimacy? Raising children? Maintaining external relationships? Making financial decisions? We decided to expand our concept to include other areas that were significant and ongoing in our lives. Some of these areas we developed based on history (knowing what had caused issues in the past) and others we created immediately upon coming through a situation. In either case, marriage is so much easier when you go through it with agreed-upon guidelines that you have created together.

We are not going to provide you with a list of rules to incorporate into your marriage. Rules will be as unique as the couples that create them. No two personalities are identical, nor are any two marriages. As an example, Tara and I love nothing more than spontaneity. Excessive structure or routine drive us both crazy. We have friends who shudder at the way we turn on a dime or run off and do something on the spur of the moment, but that is an important aspect of our marriage that we both love. Maintaining that attitude over time became one of our first proactive rules.

Rule of Engagement: Keep the marriage interesting—never stop surprising

That particular rule might not fit your marriage at all. You might be a couple who hates surprises. The thought of not thoroughly planning an event might make you cringe. That's okay! Our rules are for us, and your rules need to suit you. The key is to create guidelines that you both agree will be good for your relationship and that you can both agree to follow.

As we've grown and changed as a couple, our rules of engagement have grown with us. This is not a document you file away but rather a living document that changes as your life and your relationship naturally evolves.

We've worked with couples on this concept for several years, helping them to create their own list. Some highly structured couples have their rules in printed form they revisit and edit on a regular basis. They add, delete or modify rules as they see fit. That works for them. Other couples treat their rules of engagement more as a guideline they discuss and agree upon in a much less formal setting. That's great too. The most important thing is to get past the assumption stage, have an honest conversation, and agree on a path forward together. Ultimately, it's about the alignment, not about the specific rules.

Rules serve no purpose if they are not enforced. I don't mean this in a punitive sense, like getting ticketed for speeding by a traffic cop. You have created these rules together – you both need to agree to abide by them. It's not about using your rules as a weapon, but rather agreeing to hold each other accountable. That could mean pulling out the official list and pointing to a rule that has been violated, or it could simply be a verbal reminder that "we agreed we would…" Your list is of minimal value if you can't both agree to honor it and to hold each other accountable. It can be hard to be called out on a rule in the midst of a heated discussion. But remembering that each rule was created for the overall long-term good of the marriage can help you to pause, take a deep breath, and honor your commitment.

Biblical Rules of Engagement

God has laid out in His Word a plan for marriage and relationships, and we can create rules of engagement for our marriages that honor and follow His patterns. There are some rules that should be shared by all Christian couples. You can see examples of these, along with the scripture that inspired them in the following:

- We will remain faithful to each other (Exodus 20:14).
- We will strive to honor God in all aspects of our marriage (1 Corinthians 10:31).
- We will honor and respect one another, considering our spouse's needs first (Romans 12:10).
- Divorce is not an option. It will not be threatened or considered (Malachi 2:16, Matthew 19:9, Ephesians 5:21).

This is not an exhaustive list but rather a reminder that scripture provides us with a great model to be followed for our marriages. As you grow in your faith, allow God's word to continue to speak to you in terms of how best to operate within your relationship.

Types of Rules

Marriage rules of engagement generally fall into two categories: situational rules and proactive rules. Situational rules determine how you behave in a given, known situation. These rules might govern how you will engage in an argument or how will you act in situations that are a part of your regular routine (e.g., I will always kiss my wife before I leave the house, I will call my husband every day when I am traveling). These are not intended to be punitive but rather exist to encourage behaviors that you have both agreed will enhance your marriage.

Vice President Mike Pence has talked about rules that exist within his marriage. As an example, he will not dine with a woman unless his wife is present. He also will not go to a party where alcohol is served unless she is with him. These rules fly in the face of our current culture. In fact, when these first were made known, the media had a heyday, calling him misogynistic and biased against women. But they are jointly created, situational rules that work for Mike and Karen Pence. You could say they have a shocking marriage!

You can probably think of several stress-inducing situations you and your spouse regularly face. Perhaps you could create a situational rule that would alleviate or even prevent the associated pain. As an example, if an argument erupts every time you leave your in-law's house, you might have an opportunity to create a rule. What are the behaviors or the root causes that lead to the conflict? What could one or both of you change that would prevent this stress? I knew a couple where the husband did not like the way his wife was treated by her father. Every time they would visit, the husband would complain about his father in law and insist that his wife stand up for herself. This was a situation that his wife had lived with since childhood. While she didn't like the way she was treated, she had come to accept it. When having the situation brought up by her husband, she would erupt with anger. Though it bothered him terribly, he learned to let it go. They weren't around her parents often. His wife had learned to live with it, he needed to as well. Their rule was there would be no judgment as to how their parents dealt with them as married adults. Either could voice frustration at their own parents, but both agreed not to point out flaws in their in-laws.

Look for negative patterns in your marriage that you would like to change. What situations cause repeated conflict? Your goal should be to eliminate those areas that cause ongoing issues. It's not about stifling the argument. It's about adapting the behavior to eliminate the need to argue.

The second category of rules are proactive rules. These transcend a given situation and are more aligned with heading toward your established vision. They may be harder to quantify, but their goal is to make your marriage better over time. These rules are very personal, and they emphasize emotions as much as they do to actions. As an example, "I will provide a safe environment for my wife and family" has associated actions but is ultimately measured by the wife's feeling of security. Likewise, "I will strive to keep fun in our marriage" could deal as much with style of conversation as it does with physical activities. These rules will evolve over the course of marriage, and that is encouraged. You change over time, so does your relationship, and so should your rules. Have rules in place that make sense for the season you are in, which you both agree move you closer to your vision.

I remember a specific evening when Tara and I went with our kids to dinner at a local restaurant. We were sitting around a big table laughing and talking and enjoying the fellowship as well as the food. As I looked over Tara's shoulder, I noticed a couple sitting in a nearby booth. I had never seen them before, nor did I know anything about them. But I watched them come in, sit down, look at their menus, and order food without ever saying a word to each other. After they ordered, they both began focusing on their phones. Their food came, and they ate in silence. I didn't sense any hostility between them; instead, there was an air of boredom surrounding them. This grieved me. Based on their age, I'm guessing they were empty nesters with nothing to talk about now their kids were gone. While I continued to enjoy my meal and laugh with my family, I kept watching to see if anything changed at their table. They may have exchanged five or six words by the end of their meal, but they were finished and paying their bill as we were still enjoying ours.

If the behaviors of this couple were rare or isolated, I probably would not have given it much thought. But watching them reminded me of so many couples that I know. I realized Tara and I would one day be empty nesters as well. This sparked a conversation when we got home. I told Tara about the couple and how sad their lack of interaction seemed. I expressed my hope that our marriage would not succumb to boredom and routine. She agreed with me and suggested that we make a new proactive rule.

Rule of Engagement: Strive to keep life together worth talking about

Admittedly, there are a lot of facets to a rule like this, but it encourages each of us to do interesting things both together and individually. We always converse at dinner and never allow our phones to take priority. To this day, if I come to the dinner table in a rough mood or find myself distracted with other issues, Tara will call me out on it. When she does, that couple immediately comes to my mind, and I find myself starting to talk about something. It may feel forced at first, but within no time, we're in the midst of an interesting conversation.

Summary

Rules of engagement are a simple tool that you can implement within your marriage. It's something that you create together with the goal of continuously improving your relationship. Over time, some rules will change, and others will be added. Periodically revisiting your rules will ensure that you are both adhering to them and will provide you an opportunity to create new rules that are pertinent to your current situation.

Start simple. Create a few rules and see how they work. Determine if you are growing closer to your shared vision for your marriage or if you are drifting away from it. If you do find yourselves drifting, discuss the behaviors that are causing your challenges and create new rules to turn that trend around.

Discussion Questions

1. Where is God in terms of your marriage relationship? What steps could you take to give Him priority?

2. Do you see the value in creating rules of engagement within your marriage? What concerns might you have? Is this concept something you can both get behind? Discuss any benefits or concerns that you might see as a couple.

3. Are there situations in your marriage you repeatedly face that might benefit from situational rules of engagement? What are they (be specific)? What might those rules look like?

4. What are some broader areas that you want to focus on in your marriage (think fun, security, stability, passion, etc.)? What proactive rules could you create to help you in this area?

CHAPTER 4
DEALING WITH CONFLICT

Some people make cutting remarks but the words of the wise are healing.

—Proverbs 12:18 NLT

When couples fall in love and plan for marriage, the last thing they typically think about is conflict. "Why would we argue? We agree on everything important…" is typically the attitude. The reality is, unless you married a clone of yourself, it is impossible for two people to live together and always share the same opinion. While in some situations having these differing points of view makes minimal difference (e.g. you can't agree on a favorite movie), there are other times when you need to be in agreement in order to move forward. Sounds easy, doesn't it? If all decisions could be made based on facts and logic, it would be. The reality is, most decisions aren't so clear cut; there are many "gray areas". We are emotional beings, and most of us struggle with pride. As a result, when we find ourselves in a dispute, we spend our time and mental energy trying to develop persuasive arguments to justify our point and bolster our defenses. We are convinced that if our spouse just *understood* what we were trying to say, the argument would simply go away. We have an unrealistic expectation that goes something like this.

"If only you will *hear and understand* my point, you will quickly realize the error in your thinking. With this newfound understanding in place, you will fall silent as you immediately begin to reflect and plan a new direction based on your sincere and enlightened change of heart. You will thank me for illuminating you in your area of darkness, and our relationship will move forward in a manner far better than before. If by some chance you don't react as I expect, it must be because you clearly *didn't hear and understand* my point. To show my commitment to our relationship, I will state my point again, only this time with more volume to better facilitate your hearing. In addition, I will offer you more specific examples to help you see the brilliance of my idea and the flaws in your perspective. I may have to repeat this process multiple times, but I am willing to do so and remain convinced that in time, you will come around."

It seems ridiculous when you see it written out that way. But the reality is, that's the way most people view an argument they are in. It doesn't have to be this way. When you fundamentally agree that you are on the same team and headed toward a common goal of continuous improvement in your marriage, it makes it infinitely easier to get through times of conflict. While you think you should do something your way, your spouse clearly thinks you should do it their way. So, who is right, and who is wrong? Though that is where our thinking naturally starts, it is an irrelevant question. The reality is both approaches may be viable. So now what? In these times, you have to honestly ask yourself a key question: Is it more important that you, as a couple, get to your defined long-term goal (vision), or is it more important that you, personally, prove yourself right in this near-term situation? If you can work together, you may find there is a new, superior solution that incorporates aspects of both of your opinions. You'll have to set your pride aside for this to be possible.

Conceding an argument is not the answer. Consider the following scenario. You find yourself in an argument with your husband. You clearly see things from different perspectives, and each of you believes that your opinion/ solution is correct. After what seems like an eternity of animated discussion, he throws up his hands and says, "Okay fine, you're right. We'll do it your way." That may be the answer you hoped for, but it isn't being expressed with the correct amount of appreciation and sincerity. You suspect he doesn't really agree with you, and that further increases your frustration and anger. Instead of seeing this as a now-resolved issue, you express your disbelief in his concession, and that leads to further fighting. "You don't really agree with me, you're just saying that..." And on and on it goes. Your original intent was to convince him to agree with you, but now you are mad because he claims that he does.

You have officially found yourselves in a no-win situation. You start out wanting to win at all costs, but even if your spouse concedes, you aren't satisfied. Nothing can be said that will end this dispute on a positive note. No matter what you agree to do, it won't feel right. To make things worse, both of you will probably steer clear of this topic in the future because of the frustration and pain you experienced during the argument. Whatever the issue was, it hasn't gone away, and it certainly hasn't been resolved. The reality is, you can't "win" an argument with your spouse, so stop trying.

Disagreements may be inevitable in a marriage, but they needn't be ugly. While your natural tendency may be to try to change the attitudes or behaviors of your spouse, the better place to start is with yourself. Ask yourself the following question: Is my goal to work through a given issue and arrive at a better place, or is it to simply prove myself right and my spouse wrong?

> Pride leads to conflict; those who take advice are wise
>
> Proverbs 13:10

Pride is a major source of conflict in many areas of life, marriage is no exception. When your spouse confronts you with an issue, your prideful reaction is to rebut the confrontation and defend yourself. From there, an argument erupts, as neither party wants to back down from their original stance. When pride is on the line, there can be no winner. Both sides will ultimately feel defeated. In a shocking marriage, individuals learn put aside personal pride and learn to take pride in their relationship. This shift of mind-set can do wonders in preventing unnecessary conflict in your marriage.

Once you've learned to do this, disagreements are no longer based on who is right and who is wrong. Partners can see a situation from different perspectives and appreciate each has value. Time and energy once spent trying to win your spouse over to your side can be now be used to gain understanding. Elements of both perspectives can be incorporated into the outcome. When this happens, you will find yourself in a better place than had you somehow won the argument. The beauty is, it can be done at a lower volume and in a shorter amount of time. Imagine walking away from a potentially heated discussion feeling great about the direction you are heading together? It's possible when humility allows you to listen and work together to get to a better place.

Pride can also prevent forgiveness. If you feel you have been wronged, hearing your spouse apologize and express remorse is not enough. Pride keeps a record of wrongs, a mental scoreboard tracking how many times you have been hurt and to what degree. The reality is, your spouse is keeping a similar list of their own. As the lists increase on both sides, it clearly becomes harder and harder to get back to zero. Unresolved issues flair up with each new argument, escalating feelings far beyond what the topic at hand may deserve.

Jesus provides the example of how we should treat our spouse with forgiveness and humility. Does Jesus hold a grudge when we sin against Him? No. Does Jesus withhold forgiveness when we commit the same sin over and over? No. Does Jesus stop loving us when we put our needs first and act without considering Him? Still no. We are all called to become more Christlike in our lives, which extends to our marriages.

> Then Peter came to Jesus and asked, 'Lord, how many times shall I forgive my brother or sister who sins against me? Up to seven times?' Jesus answered, 'I tell you, not seven times, but seventy-seven times'.
>
> Matthew 18:21–22 NIV

As you develop a heart and attitude of humility and forgiveness, you will find that many arguments can be avoided altogether. When they do occur, there should be no lasting, hard feelings as forgiveness is offered and accepted.

Your Opinions Will Differ

Your goal should not be to simply avoid conflict, but rather to learn to respect your spouse's perspectives and opinions. It is critical you have mutually agreed upon a common vision and foundation for this to be possible. But with these in place, you can actually take conflict and turn it into a blessing.

> As iron sharpens iron, so one person sharpens another
>
> Proverbs 27:17 NIV

Friction and conflict within any meaningful relationship is inevitable. Just as the verse in Proverbs suggests, it is the violent interaction between two pieces of iron that causes sharpening. When this happens, sparks fly, small particles are removed from each surface and newly honed, more effective surfaces result.

I once had a boss tell me, "If you and I agree on everything, I have no need for you whatsoever." There was much wisdom in that but hearing a perspective that is different from our own can sometimes be difficult, especially if this falls into an area that we feel strongly about. It takes effort to hear such a message with an open mind and to give it proper consideration. Our prideful nature starts with the assumption that if I have a strong opinion on something, then I am inherently right. If your opinion differs from mine, you are fundamentally wrong. How do we overcome this natural tendency? For us, it became a foundational rule of engagement.

Rule of Engagement: We will use our energy to build up our relationship, not to tear each other down.

Sounds pretty basic, right? It is. But basic is not necessarily easy. Start with increasing your personal self-awareness. What is the motivation behind the point you are trying to make? Are you trying to improve the marriage, or are you seeking personal gain at the expense of your spouse? Remember, you can't win an argument. When your focus is on building the relationship, you'll find yourself in fewer heated discussions.

Sometimes you can derail an argument before it really gains steam, perhaps in a humorous manner. Let me give you an example.

I came home after a two-week international business trip. While I was thrilled to see Tara and the kids, I was exhausted from jetlag and admittedly frazzled. More than anything, I just wanted a peaceful family dinner with some casual conversation. Tara, on the other hand, had been dealing with our two sons the entire time by herself. She looked forward to getting a break by having me re-enter the family and resume helping her with parenting. Clearly our perspectives were not aligned at this point.

We all sat down to eat and began talking about our time apart. It was great to be reunited, but the reality is we both had considerable frustration just under the surface. As the meal went on, the boys started misbehaving and fighting with one another. In my exhausted state, it really grated on my nerves. I scolded them several times, but their behavior only continued to get worse. Tara seemed oblivious to their actions, which frustrated me further. As things escalated between the boys, one slammed his fist down on the table accidently causing some food to fly onto his brother, which caused them to get more out of control. Finally, out of sheer desperation, I looked at Tara and said rather loudly, "Would you please do something?" She looked at me, her eyes got big, and she calmly replied, "Okay. I will." At that point, she flicked a spoonful of mashed potatoes she was about to eat directly into my face.

I don't know who was more shocked, the boys or me. Their conflict immediately ceased and they both pointed at me with mashed potatoes falling from my nose and burst into outrageous laughter. I looked at each of them in turn then said, "Oh yeah? How about this?" I then flung a spoonful of food at each of them. At that point, it was game on and turned into a full-blown food fight right there in our kitchen. I'm sure the neighbors probably heard the yelps and laughter emanating from our home. It took a while to clean up the mess, but we all pitched in and got it done. Tara's unexpected reaction broke the negative momentum and refocused all of our perspectives A situation that was turning ugly suddenly became a memory that our boys fondly recall twenty years later.

Differing Styles

It's interesting. If you were to play a game with your spouse, you would agree upon the rules before you began. Monopoly is a game where many families have created "house rules" like taking double money if you land on Go or collecting huge cash bonuses if you land on Free Parking. You may have been raised playing the game a bit differently, but ultimately you and your spouse would agree on which rules to accept before you began playing. The reality is, conflict is much like Monopoly. Every family has its own rules and norms about how they argue and resolve conflict. But unlike Monopoly, few couples ever address these differences prior to finding themselves in an argument.

Like most couples, Tara and I came into our marriage from very different family cultures. This was not something that we ever really discussed, so we never considered the implications of our upbringing on our relationship. In many instances, the cultures in which we were raised were in direct conflict with one another. One of the earliest examples of this to emerge was in the manner and style in which we argued.

Growing up in my household, there were disagreements and differences of opinion between various members of the family, but I seldom, if ever, heard raised voices or shouting. If someone was bothered by something someone else had done, they would openly voice their concern. Conversations could get intense and very focused but typically would not end until there was some form of agreement that satisfied all parties (at least on the surface). Since that is how I was raised, I assumed this was how all families dealt with conflict.

I brought this set of beliefs and behaviors into our marriage. When something bothered me, I would communicate the issue as soon as possible. Based on my upbringing, my expectation was that we would work through the issue and reach some form of resolution. If Tara chose not to respond, I naively assumed she was in agreement. The mere act of getting my concerns off my chest made me feel better and allowed me to move on. From my perspective, we didn't argue very often.

In contrast, Tara's family handled conflict in a completely different manner. Two-way confrontation was not the norm. Her father had a strong temper and would openly yell at his wife and daughters. When one of them was angered or offended, the typical response would be to internalize the issue and go off by themselves hoping it would simply go away over time. Hurt feelings might eventually go away, but in the meantime members of the family could go for days without speaking to the one that had offended them. Stomach ulcers and other stress-induced conditions were common across her family. Just as I had done, Tara assumed what she experienced to be the way of all families.

When you bring two such different conflict styles together with no advance planning or agreeing on the rules, fireworks are sure to occur. While getting things off my chest made me feel better it had the opposite effect on Tara. She would take my words as criticism and silently internalize them letting them build up over time much like a pressure cooker. My comments or complaints would essentially turn the heat up on her feelings, but she would not say anything in the moment. To me, no reaction meant there was no problem, but that was far from reality. When a pressure cooker's relief valve blows, all the pressure that's been building up suddenly comes spewing out. That was Tara.

Imagine my surprise when (from my perspective) I would do or say something seemingly minor, only to watch her go ballistic. I didn't understand that my comment was proverbially the straw that broke the camel's back. Once she began venting, I would hear about every infraction and offense that I had committed since our last argument. "And another thing" became the most dreaded words I could hear from her. Arguments escalated quickly. I found myself matching her anger and intensity out of some instinctive sense of self-defense. It was not uncommon that after these arguments, we would each be so frustrated and angry we would storm out of the room and not speak about it (or anything else) for a few days.

After one such nasty argument, Tara got so over-whelmed that she grabbed her car keys and coat and left the house. As I heard the garage door closing behind her, I panicked. She had just driven off, leaving me at home with our kids. Where was she going? When would she come back? Would she come back? I tried to call, but she didn't answer. The worst possible thoughts ran through my mind, and I had no idea what to do. When the inevitable "where's mom?" question came from the kids, I nearly broke down. Several hours later, she came back in the house. She walked right past me but told our son that she had "needed some alone time" and simply gone to see a movie. While I was relieved she was back, I was now furious she had left me in that manner. Anger bred cruel actions that bred more anger. It was a dangerous cycle. Our arguments began to run together. It got to the point where Tara's breaking point became less and less. What we didn't realize in our youthful years of marriage is that an argument not effectively resolved is an argument still occurring.

Our fighting was becoming unbearable and neither of us wanted to carry on in this manner long term. One day, in between spats, we agreed to sit together and talk about our situation. We agreed to take turns talking and to respectfully hear each other out. We spoke of what made us angry and how we felt when we were disrespected by the other. It is unrealistic to think a conversation of this nature could take place in the heat of conflict. In what I now realize was a moment of God-inspired wisdom, we started to make a list of specific actions that trigger the anger in each of us. We talked about these items and explained the details and feelings behind them. We asked questions of each other to make sure we had a clear understanding of each concern. Most importantly, we revisited the fundamental agreement we had previously put in place. We were both in our marriage for the long haul; divorce was out of the question and off of the table. With that in mind, we came to realize while we would still argue, we knew that we would work to find a way to make up and resolve things. That was huge.

Rules of Engagement for Arguments

Most marital conflicts take the form of verbal arguments. While we may not be throwing physical punches at our spouse, our choice of words can cause lasting damage. It is in our fallen nature to strike back when we are injured. If your words hurt me, my base instinct is to one-up you with an even more critical attack. You've probably experienced the angst of being in an argument like this, one that continues to escalate until one partner breaks or walks away. In time, apologies may be made, but the scars from harsh words inevitably remain. Creating rules of engagement that are specific to conflict can minimize the lasting effect of unkind words.

Our rules of engagement became an agreement, but much more importantly a mind-set that we both agreed to abide by in future disputes. Creating this list took considerable time and effort and has continued to evolve over the years. It required each of us to learn and implement new behaviors. While not easy at first, over time these behaviors have become second nature to us.

Rules are meaningless if they are not enforceable. If you've ever watched an NBA game, you will see ten players on the court in heated competition. Arms and legs are flailing, and you can see the level of intensity being experienced by all involved. But something incredible happens when you hear a whistle blow. All players stop what they're doing, walk away from one another and wait to hear the details of the infraction that was called. This only works because they have all agreed to play by a given set of rules. One of these is that when the whistle blows play stops. Once they have determined what went wrong, they resume play again.

Marital disputes can operate under similar rules. In our case, we agreed that even in the midst of a heated discussion, either of us can call a foul if someone crosses a preestablished line. Because we are both committed to this agreement, calling foul causes us to pause, take a deep breath, and acknowledge the infraction. Oftentimes, this is accompanied by an apology, which confirms our mutual commitment to each other as well as to the rules. Just taking this pause in the midst of an argument can reset our emotions. Far too often, as things escalate, cruel words are spoken. This approach stops the argument temporarily before it gets out of hand. It took commitment and discipline at first, but over time it became a habit. Thirty plus years later, we still argue, but we continue to abide by these rules.

The following is a portion of the rules we created for dealing with conflict. These were created for us and our unique personalities and relationship. Feel free to use any of these as they are, or use them as a starting point as you go through this effort with your spouse:

Rule of Engagement: Divorce is not an option and will never be used as a threat

This was our first rule of engagement and became the cornerstone for all future rules. It reminds us that we are ultimately on the same side. While arguments still occur, we know we both want the best for our relationship, and conflict properly resolved should lead to a stronger relationship.

Rule of Engagement: If something is really troubling one of us, we need to either let it go or bring it up as soon as possible

Given a little time, certain frustrations will just go away. There's more angst created by bringing up some small issues than just letting them dissolve on their own. But you must truly let them go. If after a short period of time the issue is still bothering you, then it needs to be brought up. For us, a given conflict was now focused on a timely, specific issue and no longer a laundry list of past frustrations.

Rule of Engagement: Eliminate absolutes from our language

Certain words and phrases escalate an argument, while others tend to subdue it. We agreed to drop words like *always* and *never* (e.g., "You never pick up your socks..." or "You always leave the garage door open..."). Nothing puts a person more on the defensive than hearing words like "You never..." or "You always..." As soon as these accusations are made, your mind immediately goes to an exception where that was not the case, destroying the credibility of the accuser and intensifying the argument.

As an example, when Tara told me, "You always leave your socks on the floor," my mind immediately recalled the recent night when I took them off and intentionally put them in the clothes hamper. Because of that memory, I believed her accusation was unfounded. Therefore, I had the right and the responsibility to set her straight. In spite of my strong evidence proving her wrong, the argument was far from over. She had a legitimate complaint that my socks ended up on the floor far too frequently. My anger didn't stem from defending my slovenliness but rather from the word *always*. As we talked this through, we agreed that I should pick up my socks and that she had the right to become frustrated when I failed to do so. We both felt somewhat ridiculous at the energy we had put into an argument when we realized we were on the same side.

Rule of Engagement: Use less you words and more I words

If I am accused of something, my natural initial instinct is one of denial. But if Tara tells me that my actions cause her to feel a certain way, I feel compelled to listen. Think of this one in conjunction with the previous rule. Shift the statement from "You never pick up your socks" to "I get frustrated when I have to pick up your socks so often." This is a simple yet powerful rule. When I'm accused, I get defensive. If I learn that my actions are hurting or frustrating Tara, I am prompted to change my behavior.

Rule of Engagement: Focus on the problem and not the person

Pointing out the frustration caused by my socks constantly being on the floor is legitimate. Calling me a slob transcends the problem and becomes a personal attack. Just like in a courtroom, words may be stricken from the record, but they can't be unheard. There's no place for belittling or name-calling in a spousal dispute. That will never lead you to a better place.

Rule of Engagement: Know and look to the heart of each other

Many arguments begin with a misunderstanding. It could be that something was misstated or misheard. If I've said something that hurts Tara, I want her to first consider my motivation and my nature. Is my heart one that would intentionally wound her with my words? If it is not, I hope to get the benefit of the doubt or at least be given the opportunity to explain myself. A good tool for this is to say something like "What I hear you saying is that…" That allows for an opportunity for the other to either verify or clarify what the original intentions were. It's amazing how often in the heat of an argument that what is said is not what is heard.

Rule of Engagement: Don't go to bed mad, but do allow time for resolution

> And don't sin by letting anger control you. Don't let the sun go down while you are still angry for anger gives a foothold to the devil.
>
> Ephesians 4:26-27 NLT

When we first created this rule, it simply stated "Don't go to bed mad." That seemed to align with scripture, and I wanted to resolve every conflict immediately - then kiss and make up. But the rule didn't account for our personalities and the different ways in which we process information. While I can turn on a dime and change my mind, Tara needs to take some time to absorb and process what has been discussed. We added "allow time for resolution" to help us respect each other's needs. I now have confidence when Tara walks away from an argument we will come to resolution, and she feels the freedom to take the time she needs to process before coming to a conclusion.

Know What You're Arguing About

There are many times couples find themselves in a dispute without really understanding the core issue. Having rules of engagement can help to rectify or even prevent these situations. Here's an example of how conflict might occur in a relationship without rules of engagement.

John is an executive at an insurance company. He spent his afternoon on an extended phone meeting with his boss who lives in another city. The boss is upset with the overall performance of the company but has been taking much of his frustration out on John. From John's perspective, he has been berated and criticized for almost every decision and action that he's made for the last quarter. When he finally gets off the phone, he feels like he's been run through the wringer, can't do anything right, and honestly fears for his job. He just wants to get home and leave his frustration at the office.

John's wife, Sue, has been home with her two teenage kids all day. She feels like she has spent her entire day nagging the kids to finish their chores. The fact that it is late afternoon and many of these items remain undone leads her to feel disrespected and unappreciated as a mom. It seems nobody listens to her, and she is at the end of her rope. As she begrudgingly gives in and starts a load of her daughter's laundry, John walks in the back door. She verbalizes the first thought that comes into her head, "Did you remember to go by the store and get the trash bags like I asked you?" she asks John.

Boom!

My guess is you can create a mental picture of the next ten or fifteen minutes of their verbal exchange. Within moments of John's arrival home, Sue complains "You never do what I ask you to." She's essentially poured gas on that fire. John yells back, "Nothing I do is ever good enough for you." And from there, it gets ugly. Here's the point. John and Sue find themselves in a nasty, heated argument within moments of coming together. Over what? The reality is, it's not about trash bags.

Had John and Sue established their own rules of engagement prior to this, either one of them could have called a foul to assess what they were actually arguing about. After a cooling-off period (just a few minutes), Sue might express she could get the trash bags later when she runs to the store. John could apologize for forgetting and begin to tell her about the nightmarish conversation with his boss that distracted him. Sue could empathize and apologize for jumping on him.

She could then go on to tell John about the frustrations she had dealing with teen defiance all day. Now instead of heading off into separate rooms no longer speaking, they might just decide to sneak off without the kids and have a drink together where they could further unload their respective frustrations and come to laugh at the situation they averted. And while they're out, they could grab trash bags!

It is critically important to establish guidelines for conflict during a time of peace. Learn which conflicts are worth working through and which have no real value. If there is benefit to your differences of opinion, you can learn to get both sides expressed effectively and reach a mutual agreement. When there's nothing to be gained in an argument, recognize this early and save the emotional energy for something more proactive.

Keeping the Right Perspective

There is a difference between averting conflict and avoiding it. As hard as you might try to keep an argument from happening, sometimes it's simply unavoidable. The key is to learn to fight fair and not do any lasting damage with your words or actions. Effectively dealing with conflict is about maintaining a long-term perspective. Knowing that you, as a couple, are both completely committed to the relationship allows you to get through the tough days. Even in the midst of a nasty argument, you know you'll make it through, and things will get better once again. The danger of losing sight of your commitment to each other is you can get caught up in the moment and begin to think, say, and do things you will later regret.

When long-term perspective is lost, the relationship can quickly veer into a downward spiral. I know of couples that have lost their ability to see anything objectively. Arguments are not resolved and begin to run together. Walls have formed that are so high and thick that they no longer see their partner for who they really are. Instead, they only see problems and issues. She no longer sees the man she loves; she sees only the man who lied to her. He doesn't see his bride; he sees the woman who insists on controlling him. These points may be valid, but the priority has shifted from the relationship to the problem. Neither takes the time to remember that this was the person with whom they fell in love and committed to spend the rest of their life. Instead, all that is seen is a thin veneer of fault and badness. Over time, that veneer becomes a solid object that contains none of the goodness and blessing that once existed.

Summary

Conflict is inevitable, but it needn't be ugly or destructive. Understand that you and your spouse naturally approach conflict differently. Discuss this together and create some rules you can put in place that will keep you heading in a positive direction, even when in dispute. Learn to look past your desire to "win" an argument and strive to get to a better place. Keep the big picture in mind. Avoid words or actions that tear down the relationship. Focus on the issue at hand and not on your partner.

Discussion Topics/Questions

- In a time of peace, talk with your spouse about your attitudes toward divorce. Are you committed to your marriage for the long run? Make that vow to one another. When conflict arises, remind yourself and each other of your vow. Knowing you are ultimately on the same side goes a long way toward resolution.
- What is your natural approach toward conflict? Do you avoid it or address it head-on? How does that compare with your spouse?
- Think back to past arguments you've had with your spouse. What are some key words or phrases you heard that really frustrate you?
- Begin your individual list of rules of engagement for conflict situations. Share them with your spouse. Are there three or four points you can both agree to? Write these down and commit to abide by them during your next conflict.
- Agree what each of you will do when the other calls foul during an argument. Commit to doing your best at honoring that.

CHAPTER 5

WEATHERING LIFE'S STORMS

Consider it pure joy, my brothers and sisters, whenever you face trials of many kinds, because you know that the testing of your faith produces perseverance. Let perseverance finish its work so that you may be mature and complete, not lacking anything.

James 1:2–4 NIV

In 2011, National Geographic launched the television show called Doomsday Preppers[5]. Each episode focused on individuals or families preparing for some type of future cataclysmic event. While the nature of their concerns varied widely, from total government

---

5   https://www.nationalgeographic.com/tv/shows/doomsday-preppers

collapse, to global medical pandemics and massive natural disasters, they all had one thing in common. They were dedicated to preparing for a future state where safe food, water, and shelter would not be commonly available. In 2020 many of these fears came to life with the Covid-19 global pandemic. In the early days of the crisis, people went crazy trying to buy toilet paper and hand sanitizer. Suddenly, everyone was trying to stock up and there were no supplies to be found. Preppers did not have this problem.

None of us can know what will happen tomorrow, but there are things we can and should do to prepare our marriage to weather the inevitable storms of life. Weather-related storms range in size and severity; some are forecasted while others just pop-up out of nowhere. No matter where you live, you have surely endured some type of storm. The storms we face in life and in our marriages act very much the same.

James 1:2 uses the phrase, "Whenever you face trials." Not *if* you face trials but *whenever* you face trials. James knew that all of us would encounter hardship, so his encouragement is to "consider it joy" because God is going to use those experiences to grow our faith. In marriage, you need to simultaneously rely on God and support your spouse during such trials. In a time of calm, you can create rules of engagement that will help you remember that you are a team headed toward a common goal. You can build your marriage on a firm foundation so that you can support each other during times of individual weakness and together seek the joy that only God can provide.

Tara and I have been through our share of storms, big and small. Today, we can look back and see how God used those trials to grow our individual faith and to strengthen our marriage. But in the midst of the dark moments, it was nearly impossible to see any possible benefit or experience any type of joy. I would love to tell you we had rules of engagement in place before our storms arrived, but that would be untrue. Our rules were created after we endured the storms, in an attempt to protect us from future ones.

Having a marriage built on rock will go a long way toward protecting you when storms occur. It is also helpful, once you've come through a trial, to reflect and consider what you have learned and how you can apply that knowledge to future events. These are less like "rules" and more like guidelines. Knowing that God has gotten you through tough times in the past can help you get through future trials.

Coping with the Unthinkable

October 5, 1995 was the single worst day of our lives. I was walking down the hall at work and heard my name being repeatedly-paged on the office-wide intercom. Since the intercom was seldom used, I realized something unusual was going on. As I walked into my office, my assistant looked at me in panic and told me that I needed to get home immediately. It was something about my two-year-old daughter. I didn't stick around to ask questions; I could tell by her face that this was serious. I ran from the office and headed for home. What was normally a twenty-minute drive, I accomplished in ten.

As I pulled up to our house, all I could see were flashing lights, police, fire trucks, and ambulances. Neighbors were standing in the street with their hands over their mouths. Someone pointed me toward the backyard, and I ran. Before I could even see her, I heard Tara sobbing uncontrollably. I found her in the neighbor's yard behind our home, holding our two-year-old Allison, limp and unmoving near a pond. Filled with horror and in a state of shock, I had no idea what to do, nor could I imagine what had occurred.

As the day went on, the details became clearer. Our daughter had evidently, gotten out the back door of our home, probably following our cat she saw outside. She made her way up a steep hill behind our house, walked another forty yards and fell into a pond where she drowned. Because of the distance and the hill, we were completely unaware that our neighbor even had a pond. When Tara noticed Allison was missing (within minutes), she immediately called the police and began a frantic search, only to discover the unthinkable had happened.

The days following this tragic event were a blur. Family, friends, and ministers flowed through the house bringing food and offering comfort. Their outreach and support was critical in getting us through this crisis. Over two hundred people came to the visitation and the funeral. In my numb state, I couldn't fathom the crowd. Most of these people had never even met our daughter. It wasn't until much later that I realized God had sent these people to comfort the two of us.

Reality hit once the crowds went home. Our friends and families resumed their respective routines. But life for us was forever changed. It was hard to eat, hard to converse, even hard to parent our older two children. We were angry with each other, angry with the neighbor who owned the pond, even angry at God. Okay, we were especially angry with God. Life progressed as if in slow motion.

After a couple of weeks, I returned to work and threw myself back into my job. It served as a distraction and allowed me to regain some sense of normalcy. As a stay-at-home mom, this was a luxury Tara did not have. With the older boys back in school, she faced a suddenly empty house that was a constant reminder of Allison's absence. Life was moving on for me but for Tara, it had come to a grinding halt.

In the weeks that followed, I found myself moving through the grieving process faster than Tara, which caused friction between us. While I felt sympathy for her and understood her pain, I began to resent her withdrawal from the family. Her depression led her to sleep far more than normal, leaving housework, laundry, and cooking undone. Our older boys complained that Mom didn't play with them anymore. While I missed my daughter horribly, I began to miss having a wife and a mother for our sons. As a husband, I wanted to fix the situation and make things better. But I didn't know where to start.

A couple of months after the funeral, we received a letter in the mail from an out-of-town friend. She had just learned of the accident and was sending us a belated condolence. The bulk of her letter contained scripture and words of encouragement all aimed at providing us comfort. However, toward the end of the letter, she cited a study that showed a high percentage of couples that go through the loss of a child end up getting divorced. She encouraged us to stay strong as a couple, stay close to God and to hold each other tightly throughout this season. She assured that she would be praying for us during this time.

At first, her words angered both of us. Why would anyone plant such a thought in our minds? How terribly insensitive! But as we reflected on the letter in the following days, our anger began to subside. We started to feel the spiritual prompting behind her words. When we looked at our situation honestly, we realized there were forces beginning to pry Tara and I apart. I was moving on with life and my career as best I could, but Tara seemed stuck in that tragic moment. Both of us were growing frustrated with the other because of our different ways of grieving. Our friend's letter served as a Godly reminder that our relationship was built on rock, not on sand. While this was a terrible storm, we were committed to surviving it.

We had no specific Rules of Engagement that prepared us for this season. No one plans for such an event, and no one could predict exactly how they would react if/when faced with such a situation. But we had made commitments to each other and our faith ultimately pulled us through. As time passed and healing continued, we were able to reflect and discuss how we cope with tragedy individually and as a couple.

Rule of Engagement: We will accept the people God sends into our lives to minister to us.

Thankfully, Tara and I had already developed a deep faith when Allison died. There is one big thing that we learned by living through this ordeal. We had always considered ourselves as being self-sufficient. We volunteered at church, took other people meals when in need and did other acts of "Christian service." But we never considered needing or accepting help ourselves. When we hit rock-bottom emotionally, we had no choice but to accept the love and service of people around us. It was easy to accept help from our very close group of friends and family, but God opened the door to many others that we needed as well. Lou, the youth minister from our church (whom we'd never met personally) came the day of the accident and just sat with us. He came back every day for a couple of weeks to do the same. He had no special healing words that he thrust upon us; rather, he was just there. His presence became a tremendous comfort, and a special relationship was formed. Twenty plus years later, Lou and his family are some of our closest and most trusted friends.

The advice we received from our Christian friends was for the most part welcomed and highly valuable. But there were many nonbelieving friends who wanted to help as well. One person told us of having just read *The Wizard of Oz* and how the lessons there could guide us in the days ahead. Another secular grief counselor brought us an old tennis racket. She suggested that when we were angry or down, we should take the racket out and swing it hard against a tree. Doing so would channel our negative energy through the racket and allow it to escape our bodies. The racket went straight into the trash as soon as she left our home.

Unfortunately, not all questions or advice from Christians is necessarily godly. Not long after the funeral, Tara got a phone call from a lady at our church. We didn't know her well, but she called to offer comfort. Near the end of the otherwise pleasant conversation, she asked Tara, "What sin do you think you committed that prompted God to do this?" Tara couldn't believe her ears. The lady went on to say that she needed to know so that she could make sure she didn't commit a similar sin in her own life! It is critical that you learn to discern Godly advice from worldly advice, regardless of where it comes from.

Rule of Engagement: We will discern between Godly advice and worldly advice.

In the months and years that followed, God used our tragedy in a mighty way. I began to speak to various churches and other organizations telling our story, sharing that there is no guarantee in living another day. We need to make sure that we are prepared for our inevitable demise, no matter when it comes. The experience also birthed our marriage workshops. Our loss became a springboard to invite others to accept Christ and to strengthen their marriages. I remain convinced that someday in heaven, I will meet many people who will point to the story of Allison and credit that for their conversion or for their restored marriage. Handing our crisis to God and committing to each other grew both our faith and our perseverance.

Rule of Engagement: We will use our life experiences to benefit others.

Unfortunately, trials are seldom one and done. You never know when tough times will hit. Building and maintaining a shocking marriage will equip you to handle whatever is thrown your way.

Rebuilding the Family

A couple of years after Allison's death, Tara and I had an interesting conversation during a long car ride. I remember looking at Tara and saying, "I realize we can never replace Allison. But I do believe we can and should replace the role of daughter in our lives." I knew this was God-inspired when Tara looked at me and replied, "I've been thinking the exact same thing." At a recent doctor's appointment, she had been told that she probably wouldn't be able to get pregnant again. So, we began to talk about adoption. I had spent considerable time on business in India and felt such compassion for orphaned children there who had no real hope for the future. I raised this as a possible location that we should consider, and Tara quickly agreed. We made the decision that we would adopt from India and began the process.

By now our sons were eight and eleven. Tara didn't want to have a single daughter so much younger than her siblings, so we set out to adopt sisters. We were filled with excitement as we began the process early in 1998. We filled out all of the paperwork, hosted the home visits, submitted our fingerprints, and paid the up-front fee. We even paid a premium for expedited service so we could get the addition to our family as soon as possible.

Within a couple of months, we received pictures of two beautiful little sisters named Hema and Jyothi, aged two and three respectively. We immediately agreed to accept them and began to pray for them as we awaited their imminent arrival.

That's when our new trial began. The process dragged on as we experienced delay after delay. We were told this was not unusual when adopting from India, we should just remain patient. We continued to pray for these two little girls and for our family. Every time we received word of another issue, we would become discouraged, but we firmly believed that God was in control, so we held on to His promise.

A year after we started the adoption process, we moved back to our hometown near Indianapolis. I had started my own business, and we wanted to be closer to extended family. We had just completed the design of our new custom home when we learned that Tara was pregnant! Suddenly, we were growing from a family with two kids to become a family with five. "We're going to need to build a bigger house," we both agreed. We worked with the architect and added a bedroom to the design.

Just a couple of months before the house was complete, Tara began having complications with her pregnancy and eventually miscarried. While we hadn't planned this pregnancy, the loss was indescribable. It brought up all the feelings of losing Allison, and it felt like the pain was compounded. Again, we relied on each other and on God to get through this time. We began to question God as to what was going on and why.

In the spring of 2000, we moved into our new house, complete with a bedroom decorated for our Indian girls. It felt like a fresh start. Even in the midst of the excitement and anticipation, we were still no closer to completing the adoption. While we continued to pray for the arrival of our new daughters, we received an unexpected blessing. Tara was pregnant again, and in January 2002, our son Jacob was born.

Just before Jacob's first birthday, we got word from the adoption agency that the Indian government had shut down the orphanage where Hema and Jyothi were being raised. It stemmed from a local journalistic accusation that was later proved to be unfounded. But in any case, the two little girls we considered a part of our family were taken away, never to be seen or heard of again.

To us, this was a third form of losing a child (in this case, children). Our anger and despair were greater than ever. Every time we would walk past their empty bedroom, we were reminded of the promise that never came to fruition. Maintaining our faith became an increasing challenge. This felt like an all-out spiritual conspiracy against us, and it pushed our relationship with God and with each other to the limit.

In the depths of our mourning, we were reminded that as difficult as it was, God had gotten us through our past experiences, and His promise was He would get us through this one as well. We began to come out of our individual silos of despair and once again pulled together in conversation and prayer. We accepted we would once again have three children. This season led to new rules of engagement that have served as ongoing reminder in more recent storms.

Rule of Engagement: We will trust that God can sustain us through any situation.

Rule of Engagement: We will respect and support each other as we grieve differently.

Rule of Engagement: We will keep lines of communication open between ourselves and with God even in the toughest of times

Right after we celebrated Jacob's second birthday, we received an unexpected phone call from a social worker in Washington, DC. Our adoption file had been transferred to his office, and he had identified a new little girl (from India) for us and wanted to confirm our continued interest in the process. We couldn't believe our ears! We assumed once the orphanage closed, our adoption prospects had ended. We had no idea anyone was still trying to find a child for us. While our hearts still ached for the loss of the original sisters, we immediately agreed to proceed with this new child.

Later that year, we adopted the most beautiful little girl we'd ever seen. Her birthday was also in January, just a week before Jacob's. It wasn't until we celebrated both of their birthdays for the first time that we realized "Hey, look, we have siblings aged two and three. Wasn't that the original intent?" God's ways are not always our ways. We had four children aged seventeen, fourteen, three, and two. Going back to my roots of being raised on a farm, we began to affectionately refer to them as our spring crop and our fall crop of kids. To this day, we still find ourselves praying for Hema and Jyothi. There's no way to find out what became of them, but we sincerely hope to see them in heaven one day.

Rule of Engagement: We will trust in God's plan for our lives, even when it differs from our own

We have a fantastic, tight-knit family. It's not one that we could have ever imagined or planned for, but we see it as a pure blessing from God. In times of uncertainty since this season, we have learned to trust in God even when the way forward is not obvious.

Financial Hardship

The Great Recession hit my business hard in the fall of 2007. I had built it up to a nine-person company and was beginning to be recognized as an industry leader. Our focus was on the very front-end of new product development, meaning that we helped companies to develop ideas and strategies that they could implement in the future. Over the course of a few weeks, our work suddenly dried up completely. We went from managing four to five projects at a time to zero.

Based on the hint of a forthcoming recession, our target clients stopped investing in future opportunities, opting instead to sit on their cash and spend only on near-term necessities. As a result, our company was hit much earlier than others. While the word recession was being bantered about on television and news magazines, the effects were not yet commonly seen. I had business owning friends who claimed their companies were booming. I assumed it was just a blip, and things would simply come back if I remained patient and steadfast.

The team I had assembled was like family, and I held them together much longer than I should have from a financial standpoint. By the time I let the last person go in 2008, I had gone almost six months with no revenue coming in, and payroll and other expenses going out. I'd dug a deep hole for myself. With the recession now in full swing, it was nearly impossible to see a way out.

Through renegotiation with lenders and investment by extended family members, I was ultimately able to keep the business open. But during the worst of that season, I had to put myself on unemployment for almost six months. I feared losing my house and everything else that I owned. I felt like a complete failure both as a business owner and as a husband. One day as I was going through the mail, I came across a life insurance statement. It took no time at all to realize that I was worth considerably more dead than alive. I didn't actually contemplate suicide, but horrible, negative thoughts did begin to flood my mind. Why would Tara stay with me? Didn't she deserve better? She was going through this season along with me and was aware of our unpaid bills and threatening debt collectors. Yet she had a peace and a calmness that I could not seem to muster. The last thing that I wanted to do was to ruin her demeanor by sharing my concerns and fears. Not talking about it seemed better than getting into a highly uncomfortable conversation. In reality, though my intent was to display an attitude of faith and strength, she saw right through it.

One day, I broke down in front of her. The stress was just too much for me to bear. Not only was I not being a good provider; now I was a sobbing, weak man. When I finally settled down, she looked me in the eye and very calmly asked me, "What is the worst that could happen?"—a question that infuriated me. Was she in complete denial? I looked at her in shock and responded something to the effect of "I'll tell you the worst that could happen. We can lose our house. We'll have to declare bankruptcy. Life as we know it will be over. We'll have to live under a bridge!" She sat directly across from me, put her hands on my knees, looked me right in the eye and said, "If that happens, then we'll live under a bridge together." I could never express how much that brief sentence meant to me, but it completely changed my perspective. In that moment, I was able to separate our situation, which was temporary, from our relationship, which was committed and lasting. I realized we were in this situation together, and no matter what the outcome might be, our marriage would stay intact. I no longer carried the burden alone. She shared it with me. We began to pray together and plan various contingencies. When we had nowhere else to turn and had given the entire situation to God, things began to change for the better. My phone started to ring, and work started to come back in. God had sustained us through another trial. I thank God for his provision and for Tara's inspirational faith.

Creating Rules of Engagement to Get Through Trials

I pray you never have to go through the loss of a child or severe financial strain, but every marriage will experience trials of some sort. Are you prepared? During these times, the devil wants nothing more than to separate you from your strongest supporters; God and your spouse. How many people do you know who have questioned God's very existence or turned away from Him as a result of a severe trial? Our friend's statistics were true: a high percentage of marriages do result in divorce after the loss of a child. Trials are the ploys of Satan to separate us from our base of strength. While a cord of three is not easily broken, a single cord can snap easily.

Committing to God and to your spouse, regardless of circumstance, is a critical step in preparing for an uncertain future. Just as the doomsday preppers are stockpiling food and water, you need to be preparing your heart and soul for trials you will face. When you are in the midst of hardship, these commitments will go a long way toward helping you through.

Summary

Every couple goes through trials of varying degrees. The key is to pull together during these times and to rely on God's strength rather than your own to get you through. Once you get through a given storm, reflect on it. Talk about how you handled it individually and as a couple. How well did you support one another? Did you allow others to assist you through? Working through trials can be extremely difficult, but when you get through them together, your relationship should be stronger than ever.

Discussion Questions

- What trials have you gone through as a married couple? How did they affect your relationship?
- What did you learn about yourself from the experience? What did you learn about your spouse from the experience?
- What promises does God provide that can sustain you during trials?
- What role does communication play during trials? How does it affect your communication with God? How does it affect your communication with your spouse?
- Based on what you've learned, what rules of engagement could you create that would help you in future trials?

CHAPTER 6
OUTSIDE INFLUENCES

I have some friends who have recently married. For both of them, it is a second marriage. He brings three children into the mix, and she brings two. They are the picture of a blended family. Like any newlywed couple, they have both joys and struggles. They are learning day by day and week by week what it means to be in a committed relationship. I asked them recently to define the biggest challenge in their marriage. They were unified in their response. It's the outside influences they deal with on a daily basis. Both members of this couple have to deal with an ex-spouse who shares custody of their children. Further complicating things, both of their exes have remarried, bringing another voice and opinion into their world. "If marriage were just about us, it would be easy," they said. "It's all the other people that interfere that make it tough."

Marriage might be easier if it was only the two of you, but unless you live on a deserted island, in-laws, coworkers, friends, exes, children, and others will have some level of influence in and on your relationship. Not all influences are bad. You may be aware of Godly marriages you could learn from and model, but no other relationship is exactly like yours.

Creating the New Nuclear Family

A man leaves his father and mother and is united to his wife, and they become one flesh. Genesis 2:24

This is the verse where the phrase "leave and cleave" originates. It describes a familial transition. Marriage is the beginning of a new nuclear family. The original families don't go away, but they change in terms of priority and relationship.

The first significant external influence that most couples face are former nuclear-families and new in-laws. You may know on an intellectual level that your spouse is your top priority but living that out can be challenging. Before you can become a new nuclear family, you have to extricate yourself from your old one. While this may be more applicable to a young person marrying, it still holds true to some degree as you age. As a married couple, you have to intentionally break the old bond that existed with your parents. That doesn't mean abandon, but it does mean establishing and communicating a new relationship is now being formed. In an ideal situation, parents would understand this and "let go," but that is not always the case.

As a father of two adult married sons I know it can be hard as a parent to let go. It's a strange phenomenon. One day I was Dad providing guidance and counsel, and the next day, my sons were married, and my job had suddenly changed. I saw them being strongly influenced in different directions by their wives and making decisions differently than I would have suggested. But it's no longer my place to direct. I'm still here to offer advice when asked, but I have to recognize that they are leading their own families now. As hard as this was with my sons, I can't imagine what it will be like when my daughter goes from under my wing to the wing of her future husband. But I know even now I will have to honor that new relationship.

A husband has to learn to depend on his wife and prioritize her needs and desires over those of his parents, especially his mother. This can be an early and ongoing point of contention in marriage, especially if wife and mother begin competing for his attention and his favor. Many men don't even see this happening, but I can guarantee you their wives do.

In our case, my parents would come to visit us when we lived out of state, typically for several days at a time. My mom was the type who wanted to help everyone when she could, and certainly wasn't one to sit idle. During one of their visits, Tara and I were both away at work while they were at our house. Mom noticed a small stain in the grout of our white tiled kitchen floor. She found some kind of scouring powder and an old toothbrush and began to clean. One stain led to another and the next thing you know, she had spent the entire afternoon on her hands and knees cleaning all of the grout in our kitchen.

Since they were in town, I arranged to come home from work early. After greeting me with a hug, she told me she was really tired and sore, informing me of what she had done all afternoon. While it was not something I would have noticed, I sincerely appreciated the effort. An hour later, Tara arrived home from work. I immediately told her what Mom had done, thinking she would be thrilled. To my surprise, Tara looked perturbed, but graciously thanked Mom anyway. What I perceived as my Mom being helpful, Tara saw as condemnation of her housekeeping. Whether Mom meant it that way or not, I'll never know. But I'll never convince Tara it was not a veiled criticism.

Over time, I learned one way I could support Tara was to redirect my mom when she started "helping" without first being asked. I either convinced her to do something else, or I would step in and say, "Let me do that." Even if that didn't always work, Tara appreciated my awareness and intent.

Wives are not exempt from family ties either. If a woman has had a strong father in her life, it can be very tough for her to suddenly put total trust into a new man, even when that man is her husband. In many cases, a woman may come from a situation where Daddy has provided for her every need and whim. There weren't many things she had to do without. Now that she's married, the couple may be taking several steps backward from a financial standpoint, and she may be forced to live within a budget for the first time in her life. How difficult must it be for her to deny a desire when she knows that she could fulfill it with a simple request to her father?

Perhaps it's not a financial tie that controls her. In other situations, wives have come from a domineering father to whom she could never say no. Suddenly, the desires of the husband may directly conflict with the desires of the father. She may be faced with saying no to her father for the first time in her life.

In our early years of marriage, we would travel back home for holidays. Since our parents live close to one another, we would alternate where we slept, but we would attempt to divide our time between the two families. Staying at my parent's home was comfortable (at least for me), but I hated staying with Tara's parents. Her parents had a small home with one shared bathroom and no place for privacy. We assumed it was important to them that we stayed there occasionally. It turned out that was a bad assumption. When Tara actually talked to her mom about this, it turned out the extra people staying in their home overnight made it uncomfortable for everyone. Once we discovered this, we began sleeping at my parent's house, but spending time with both. This worked out well for everyone. We tried to stop making assumptions about what others wanted from us and just outright ask them.

We discovered another issue that we had to learn to get past. Tara became a different person when she returned to her childhood home. Her attitude changed, her demeanor, even her vocabulary. Essentially, she reverted back to the person she was when she was living there under her parent's authority. I would hear her agree to things I knew she opposed and silence her opinion on issues that she felt strongly about. It drove me crazy. I would wonder who abducted my wife and replaced her with this person?

Tara would say the reverse happened when we were at my parent's house. I would become in her words "a helpless little boy" who allowed my mother to wait on me hand and foot. In hindsight, Tara's commands for me to "get up and get it yourself" should have been a clue to her frustration! As it turns out, each of us reverted back to the person and role that we had played when we were living with our parents. It's hard to establish a credible, new nuclear family if we don't consistently perform in our new roles. This duality is unhealthy in any setting, and it led to a rule that we both eventually agreed to.

These alternative behaviors are not limited to being around family. Some people struggle with wearing multiple hats, each with its own personality. They act different around church friends than they do around their non-believing friends. They act differently when around coworkers than they do their golf buddies. God made you to be who you are. Learn to be that person in all situations, so your spouse can come to know you deeply for who you really are.

Rule of Engagement: Don't let the people around us dictate who we are or how we behave.

This one was as much of an adjustment for our parents as it was for us. Before long, it became the new norm, and everyone came around.

You may not be blessed with in-laws who want the best for you as a couple. I can think of several couples that were wrecked by selfish parents who, consciously or not, undermined the marriage. In each case, the parents felt from the beginning that the chosen spouse was not good enough for their child. Through a series of ongoing comments and actions, these parents manipulated and influenced the marriage for the worse. If you find yourself in a situation like this, for the good of your marriage, run! Marriage is hard without having someone on the outside who is essentially creating a wedge between you. There may come a time when you can reestablish a relationship with appropriate boundaries, but until then, prioritize your spouse and your one-flesh union.

Keeping Children in Perspective

The presence of children can and will influence your marriage. From birth, your kids will want and demand your individual attention and show clear signs of jealousy when they see your attention diverted to others, especially your spouse. While this is natural, it should not be catered to. God has given us a specific order regarding our relationships. Our first priority is God Himself, our second is our spouse (the person with whom we've become one with), and our third is our children. That is the natural order of things. When you get your priorities out of order, things will get out of whack.

We live in a "kid-first" culture. Many parents will do anything possible to support their kids in order to ensure their long-term success. I know of one family that sacrificed financially to support their daughter on a traveling soccer team. Through her junior high through high school years every weekend was spent driving to different cities, staying in hotels, eating at restaurants. Their house was in a state of disrepair, their marriage was rough, and they had a mountain of credit card debt. In their minds they justified this by thinking their daughter would get a full scholarship to college and they would recoup their investment with the savings in tuition. The reality is, the daughter did get a partial scholarship to an out of state school, but that only brought her fees back to the level they would have paid for an in-state, public university. After two years of playing on the college team, she declared she was burned out, and dropped out of soccer completely. They had to take out high-interest loans just to help her finish school. I have to wonder if that couple had eliminated the soccer-associated travel expenses and spent some money on the occasional date night where their marriage might be today.

It's not just about money. It's also about the time and energy invested in kids. I see many couples so worn out from meeting the needs of their kids, they have nothing left for their marriage. They take the time to drive their kids to a seemingly endless list of activities but can't seem to schedule the occasional date night. I've heard many husbands bemoan the fact that their wives will do virtually anything for the kids, but when it comes time to attending to his physical needs, he is met with the "I'm too exhausted" routine. Over time, this will create an unhealthy sense of jealousy and resentment that has no place in a Godly marriage.

Rule of Engagement: We will keep each other a top priority

Keeping your spouse a top priority begins with intentionally spending time together without your children. Start when the kids are young. Find a reliable babysitter and take the occasional evening out for date night. So many couples I know have kids who are entering school age but have never left their kids with a sitter. It's not about spending more time with your spouse than with your kids, but merely spending intentional time with the person you have committed to in marriage. At some point, the kids leave home, and it's important to still have a solid relationship with the person who stays behind with you.

Part of prioritizing your spouse is understanding where they stand on different issues regarding parenting and reaching a place that works for the both of you. I had a lifelong friend who got married in his late thirties. In many ways, he was the exact opposite of his new bride. From a social and political perspective, he was extremely conservative. She, on the other hand, was very progressive in her worldviews. And yet they were a great couple. They would get into some crazy arguments over various things, but they kept their differences in perspective. Within three years of getting married, they had two lovely little girls. As the babies became toddlers, they discovered the need for some type of discipline. And that's when the conflict began. My buddy was of the firm opinion that a swat on the behind was the most effective form of correction. His wife was absolutely appalled at any form of physical discipline. Her approach was one of putting the girls in time-out and then discussing their behavior to help them realize the error in their ways. This was the first time in their marriage that their differences in approach and opinion affected lives beyond their own. Without having agreed on a philosophy and technique, they found themselves in a heated debate, in front of the girls, every time discipline was required.

One Saturday afternoon, his family along with another family (with similarly aged kids) were visiting our home. All of our six kids were in the basement with us dads, while the moms were upstairs preparing dinner. Everyone was having a good time when our other friend's little girl suddenly began crying and ran to her dad. "Suzie bit me!" she screamed as she pointed directly at my conservative friend's daughter. He immediately grabbed his daughter Suzie, turned her to face him, and asked her "Did you bite Sally?" "Yes," she calmly replied. This was not the answer he was hoping for. Had she denied it, he could have given her an idle threat to behave and moved on. So, not sure what else to do, he repeated his question, "I asked you, did you bite Sally?"

And once again, she calmly replied, "Yes." I knew that he wanted to give her a little spanking as a consequence for her behavior, but he knew the degree to which this would upset his wife. Not knowing what else to do, he finally told her not to do it again in his sternest voice. He later shared with me how disempowered this made him feel. In spite of all of the differences they had learned to manage, this was one area that really caused them friction in their marriage.

Rule of Engagement: We will be unified in our parenting approach

It's important to discuss and agree upon parenting issues before you are directly confronted with them. When the kids are young, what types of discipline are acceptable to use and under what circumstances? As the kids get older, what is your policy on visiting friends or sleepovers? In the teen years, what is the minimum age for dating? What is the curfew? How strictly will we enforce our rules and what are the consequences for breaking them? Gaining alignment with your spouse on these areas is critical, and it is much easier to achieve when you're not under the pressure of making a specific decision that has not been discussed.

Having agreed upon and communicated rules will keep your kids from going to the "easy" parent to get what they want. Kids learn early on which parent to ask for each situation. Often, parents feed this type of behavior with statements like, "Okay, but don't tell your mother" or "We'll buy this, but your father doesn't need to know." This teaches your children that their parents are not unified. It also teaches them they can play one parent against the other to serve their own advantage.

I learned to never consent to my children's requests without first asking them, "Have you asked your mother? What did she say?" If I learned Tara had already said no, I would not contradict her. If they hadn't asked her, I would either make a decision on the spot or tell them I needed to discuss the request with her first. By having discussions with your spouse during a time of no pressure, you will learn the appropriate approach for each situation.

Rule of Engagement: We will not let our kids play us against each other.

Here's an example from my youth. I was very close with my mom, especially during my teen years, and would go to her to vent on days whenever I had hit my limit of frustration with my dad. Being raised on a farm, I found myself working for and with my dad throughout my youth. While he was a great man, he was hard to please and had high expectations for the work I did for him. There were times when it felt like no matter how hard I tried; I couldn't satisfy him. During those times, more than anything else, I wanted Mom to take my side and stand up to Dad on my behalf. She would listen. She would advise. But she would never side with me against Dad. She would remind me that he was her husband, and they were a unified front. While she was sorry I was angry, I'd have to either move past it or work through my issues directly with him. Little did I know how much I would come to appreciate her example when raising teen boys of my own!

There may be legitimate times when you and your spouse don't agree on an issue, or the situation may require more discussion. We've had many situations where one of us has told our kids no and the other did not understand why. When we discuss the specifics away from the children, sometimes we will come to see the other's reasoning for denial, and other times we will collectively agree that it would be okay to change our answer to "yes" instead. If we decide something should change, the original decision maker is the one to go back and give the revised answer. Allowing the original parent the opportunity to communicate sends the message that sometimes answers change, once due consideration has been given or as more information has become available.

Avoid Toxic Influences

While we should think carefully about how we represent our spouse to others, we must also guard our hearts against what we allow others to say to us about our spouse. I know of several relationships that ended in divorce when one of the partners became immersed in a negative social environment. One friend of mine had been married for about ten years and had two young daughters. I remember his excitement when his wife took a new job at a local company. With her significant increase in pay, he was very excited about what their future would hold. But within six months of starting her job, she surprised him by filing for divorce.

In her new position, she found herself in a department filled with divorced women who had all developed bitterness toward marriage and men in general. In her early time there, she would tell "funny" stories about something her husband had done, mostly in an effort to break the ice and forge relationships. But before long, she began to get unsolicited feedback and advice from her peers. "You deserve better," "I wouldn't put up with that," even "I left my husband when he did that." Though it wasn't her original intent, her desire to fit in opened the door for unwanted opinions. Eventually, their words chipped away at the foundation of her marriage until the foundation was completely destroyed. You may have heard the old saying "Hurt people, hurt people." If you are not lifting your marriage up to serve as a light for others, you run the risk of having their darkness bring you down. We can't always control who surrounds us, but we can control what we say and believe. We need to make the protection of our marriage the highest priority. That means not tearing it down (even in humor) around others. And it means building up our spouse at every opportunity both directly and to others.

Positive Outside Influences

While avoiding toxic influences is wise, we should all seek out positive relationships that can help us grow our marriages in a God-honoring manner.

Tara and I led a life group through our church, with six or seven couples that regularly attended. The group became very close in terms of sharing and building relationships. One week, someone invited a friend to attend our group. We didn't know very much about this lady other than she was separated from her husband and raising a son from a prior marriage on her own.

She began to attend each week and over time began to open up to the group. One week during prayer time, she told us that she and her estranged husband had decided to file for divorce. Having been through this once before, she expressed the pain and hassle associated with the process. She asked us as a group if we could pray for her divorce, specifically that it would go as smoothly and efficiently as possible.

In that moment, the Spirit moved within our group, which led me to reply, "I'm sorry. We will not pray for your divorce. However, we will pray for your reconciliation and for your future as a family." There was stunned silence across the group, yet everyone knew this was what we were called to do. Her response was one of defiance, "I think we're way past that. I would just appreciate if you would all just pray that we get through this as simply as possible."

At that moment, another member of the group asked if he could invite her husband to the following week's gathering. She replied that she didn't care but didn't think he would ever consider attending. The following week, he surprised us all by showing up. He had an attitude, but he was there. I'll never forget how he sat in a chair, removed from the group, with his arms crossed defiantly across his chest. We held our study as normal then went into prayer time. His request was identical to hers from the week before, and our response to him was the same, "Sorry. We're just not going to pray for that."

This continued on for several weeks, with both of them in attendance but sitting on opposite sides of the room. Each week we would pray fervently for their reconciliation. In time, we began to sense a softening between them. A few weeks later and they began to sit beside each other. Fast forward a couple months and our life group spent a Saturday moving all of his possessions back into their home! God completely restored their marriage and went on to equip them to become leaders in the church. That was almost fifteen years ago. Now this couple has grandchildren, and they live an incredibly blessed life. And it's all because a group of people felt led to pray for their marriage instead of against it. With prayer, they were able to change their vision from one of separation and divorce to one of living together in a strong rebuilt marriage. Their foundation is firmly built on rock today, and they have become an inspiration to many other couples that are struggling.

Summary

Marriage would be easy if it were just the two of you. But you have other people that influence your relationship. Parents, in-laws, children, ex-spouses, friends and coworkers all have some effect on your relationship. The key is to learn to identify those that are positive and those that are negative. Learn from those that can benefit you and shield yourselves from those that will tear you down either knowingly or unintentionally. Prioritize your marriage relationship. Help your children to understand the importance it holds in your lives. Be united in your parenting approach and never let your children play you against each other.

Discussion Questions

- Who are the people that have the biggest influence on your marriage? What influence is positive? Negative?
- What specific challenges do you have with your in-laws? What guidelines could you put in place as a couple to minimize these issues?
- Are there are any areas of parenting where you need to align your views? What issues would you like to be unified in as your children get older?
- What can you do to show your children that your marriage is a priority?
- Think of some specific examples where your kids tried to use you against your spouse. How did you handle that? How should you have handled that?
- Imagine you are with a group of your (same sex) friends. They begin belittling their spouses in a humorous manner. What is something you could do or say that would prevent you from joining in?

PART 3

REINVIGORATE YOUR MARRIAGE

CHAPTER 7
KEEP THE SPARK ALIVE

The rules described so far have dealt with minimizing a negative situation, be it conflict or grief. But proactive rules can also be established in your marriage to keep things going well. Passion and physical interest in your spouse come easily in the early years of marriage. But as life progresses, kids come into the picture and career demands increase, this can be an area that is often neglected. Intentionality in this area is critical to maintain a shocking marriage.

I was an Eagle Scout, and as a part of my Scout experience, I learned how to start a fire using natural materials. Through that process, I came to understand it takes considerable effort to create a spark. Once you've got a spark, you do everything possible to keep it alive until you can convert it first into ember and ultimately into an actual flame. You have to gently blow on an ember to keep it glowing until the adjoining material catches fire. It's an involved process requiring you to pay close attention to what you're doing and react based on what is happening. Sometimes the environment around you makes it easier (think dry materials) and sometimes considerably harder (think wet materials on a really windy day). As a determined Scout, the goal was to get a fire going regardless of the conditions. Once the fire was lit, there was a tremendous feeling of satisfaction and accomplishment.

To this day, one of my favorite parts of camping is waking up in the morning and reigniting the remnants of the campfire from the previous night. While the fire may appear to be completely burned out, I will dig around in the charred wood and under the ash looking for an ember. Once I find one, I know that with some effort, I can get the fire going again. I'll gather and add fresh kindling, then get down on my knees and gently blow on the ember. When I see it begin to turn from ash white to glowing red, I know I'm making progress. After a short while, the fire is going again, wood can be added, and it will burn all day if I just keep tending it.

Like a campfire, there are times when our marriages are blazing hot and times when the heat subsides. When distractions in life pull us away from our spouse, the embers get buried. If we're committed to staying together, the fire never goes out completely, and with some effort, we can work to get the fire going again.

Satisfying Unmet Needs

We all have needs. Basic physical needs (e.g., food, water, clothing, and shelter) are required for survival. A starving person will do things once inconsiderable in order to get nourishment. Once our basic needs have been met, we also have emotional needs (e.g., acceptance, love, friendship, empathy) and spiritual needs (e.g., the innate desire to connect with something much larger than ourselves). While we may be able to satisfy our own physical needs, we have to look beyond ourselves to satisfy our emotional and spiritual needs.

Early on in marriage, it is easy and natural to focus on your partner's needs. You would do anything for them during the honeymoon phase. Over time, the newness begins to dissipate and comfort and routine slip in. The attention often shifts from focusing on your partner's needs to assessing your own unmet needs. You begin to mentally evaluate your spouse in terms of how well they are pleasing you and fixate on areas where they are letting you down. Disappointment sets in, and instinctively, you begin to crave fulfillment, either consciously or subconsciously.

A woman whose emotional needs are not met within marriage may turn to friends, social media, or movies. Eventually, she may become vulnerable to the attention of other men, seeking to fill the void that exists in her own marriage.

For men, the need is typically not emotional but more often physical (sexual). Seventy percent of men aged eighteen to thirty-five admit to having been on an Internet pornography site within the last month. The sad truth is there is no measurable difference between Christian men and men who are not believers in this regard. Many justify this outlet as filling a void their wife no longer satisfies.

I'm not excusing any of these behaviors. Sin is sin, no matter what might lead you to it. But staying focused on your spouse and their needs is one powerful way to minimize the temptations they might otherwise face. Shifting the focus back from self to partner takes commitment and effort. It's neither easy nor natural, but it can be learned. Focus on your own behaviors and work hard to fulfill the needs of your partner. It's an interesting phenomenon. The more you work to meet their needs, the more your own needs will ultimately be met.

Fighting Complacency

We own an English bulldog. He's lazy, he snores, he drools, and he can clear a room when he passes gas. We also have a cat. She's a typical cat, showing no interest in anyone who wants to play with her and ceaselessly tormenting any non-cat lovers who happen by. We got our bulldog puppy when the cat was about eight years old. These two have developed an interesting relationship. While they were mortal enemies at first, they don't really fight anymore, they simply coexist. The cat will be in the room with us until she sees the dog approaching, then she casually exits for another part of the house. If the dog happens to notice her, he might growl a little. But for the most part, that requires too much energy. They appear to have agreed upon a mutual avoidance strategy. Both feel they deserve to be in the room, but they choose not to be around each other.

While amusing in the animal world, it's very sad when this behavior is replicated in marriage. Too many couples live this way, coexisting in the same space, moving from room to room while avoiding eye contact. They may be past fighting, certainly past loving but stay together out of habit or convenience.

This does not happen overnight. Relationships have natural ups and downs. Couples go through phases where they are crazy about each other, and through phases where they drive each other crazy. Shocking marriages look past the momentary feelings and rely on the promised, long-term commitment. Beyond that they are proactive when they find themselves edging toward complacency and do something to reinvigorate the relationship.

It's natural to fall into patterns of laziness and routine with your spouse because it's comfortable, predictable and, let's face it, easy. Comfort and predictability may sound desirable, but when carried to an extreme, lead to boredom and discontent, which are very dangerous. Marriages in this condition are extremely vulnerable to others who might offer more excitement and attention. Let me state it clearly.

Complacency Is the Enemy of a Shocking Marriage!

It's amazing how much effort you put on making a great impression on strangers or people you barely know. There's much truth in the old saying: "You only have one opportunity to make a great first impression." First impressions go a long way and last a long time. Your spouse made a first impression of you when you met. In marriage, you make continued impressions on your spouse every time you're together. If your ongoing actions don't support their first impression, their perception of you will change over time. This can be a positive or a negative – it's really up to you.

There is beauty in the comfort that comes with an ongoing, intimate relationship. You should be able to say and do things in front of your spouse that you would never consider doing in front of others. But when comfort becomes complacency, or when you stop caring what impression you are making, your relationship will begin to erode.

Picture this. Wives, you are at a business function with your husband. You stand loyally at his side throughout the evening and thoroughly enjoy the charm, the warmth, and the conversation that he exhibits with everyone he encounters. You see a facet of him that you absolutely adore, a side that caused you to fall in love in the first place. But you feel torn. You ask yourself, "Is this the same man who won't look up from the television when I'm trying to talk with him at home? Is this charmer the same guy who burps at dinner and grunts a reply when I ask a question? What happened to the man I married?"

Flip side. Husbands, you attend a social charity event with your wife. You are quite taken back when she emerges from the bathroom looking like a model. She's dressed to kill. Her hair is stunning. Her makeup perfectly applied. You couldn't be prouder to be her husband as you notice the other men taking a second glance at her throughout the evening. Having the most beautiful wife at the party makes you stand a little taller. You feel confident and aroused at the same time. The next day at work, you can't stop thinking about her and can't wait to get home to be with her physically. However, when you walk in the house, your fantasy is shattered. She's wearing sweatpants, a ratty T-shirt, and her hair is a mess. She tells you how hard she's been working at deep cleaning the bathrooms all afternoon.

Why is it that we act and dress for success with mere acquaintances but take our spouse for granted so much of the time? Why do we care so much about what others think while completely ignoring how we portray ourselves to the person we love the most?

Let me share with you a great real-life positive example. Several years ago, my sister-in-law and her kids were visiting from out of state, and we had been playing around our pool all day. My brother, her husband, was due to fly in from a business trip and join us that evening. As late afternoon approached, she quietly slipped away leaving her kids in the pool with our family. She went into the house, showered, put on nice clothes, makeup and did her hair. When she came back outside, I was surprised at her transformation and asked her if they were going out somewhere? I'll never forget her response, "No. But Jim (her husband) will be here soon, so I did this for him." "Why?" I asked. Without hesitation, she replied, "He's been traveling all week. He's been around beautiful, professional women at the office, and I want to look my best for him when he gets here." She didn't do this out of fear or paranoia, but with a sense of joy and anticipation.

My brother and sister-in-law have a shocking marriage, and it's one that Tara and I have tried to model in many ways. There's nothing wrong with dressing up and acting your best for other people, but you should be willing to do that for your spouse upon occasion as well. A solid relationship should be one where you can truly be yourself and feel both safe and comfortable. However, you must avoid becoming so comfortable and self-centered that you begin to put your own needs ahead of your partner's. A healthy relationship requires a balance in this area. What my sister-in-law showed us was that she gave her husband intentional priority over the other relationships that surrounded her. This resulted in a new rule of engagement for us.

Rule of Engagement: I will not take my spouse or their needs for granted

Prioritizing the Family

Giving your spouse priority is difficult, especially once kids enter the picture. We live in a kid-focused culture where lives often revolve around the desires, needs, and schedules of our children. Obviously, there are seasons where this may be required. A newborn will not patiently wait for Mom and Dad to finish their conversation before loudly declaring their hunger. But as kids get older and gain self-sufficiency it is important they learn to respect that mommy and daddy need time together. I've heard it said that "good kids don't make a great marriage, but a great marriage can make good kids." One of the greatest gifts you can give your kids is a solid marriage where mutual love and respect are consistently modeled.

I'm amazed how few couples set aside any time for date nights without the kids. Many couples we've met have *never* gotten a babysitter! In our conversations, it was often the mother who was reluctant to commit to a date night, mentioning the guilt she would feel leaving the kids behind even for an evening.

This attitude can communicate a variety of messages. The husband hears, "While you used to be my primary focus in life, now that we have children, you are being placed on the back burner. I'll get back to you someday." The children hear, "You are the most important people in Mommy's life. Daddy is here to help me meet all of your needs." And those outside of, but close to, the marriage hear, "I needed him to give me these kids. They're my everything now." All these messages are troubling and outside of God's design for marriage.

Your marriage thrives when you have distinct priorities. First is your relationship with God, second is your relationship with your spouse, and third is your relationship with your kids. When any of these get out of order, problems arise. In the pool example, my sister-in-law left the kids behind with Tara and I when she went in to change. She knew the kids were safe, and she made the choice to stop playing with them to prepare herself for her husband. Her priority was clear! Helping your children understand your priorities is critical. It allows them to see where they fit in in terms of the natural order of things. Our kids knew that if Tara and I were in a serious conversation, they needed to wait to interrupt to get our attention. I appreciated when Tara would look at them and say, "Mommy and Daddy are talking right now. If this is not an emergency, you need to wait." It communicated to me that I was her priority, and it communicated to the kids that our relationship was of key importance.

Just as setting aside regular time for a date night is important, setting aside smaller amounts of time on a more frequent basis is also important. One thing that we did was implement an ongoing event that we called Martini Mondays. This amounted to setting aside thirty minutes when I got home from work on Monday when we would sit on our front porch, the back deck, or somewhere else intentional and have Mommy and Daddy time. We might drink a martini, or it might be a glass of iced tea, but our goal was making time to talk and reconnect. Before long, the kids learned that we did not want to be disturbed during that time, and they came to respect it. Traditionally, there's so little to like about Mondays, but we made it our favorite day of the week.

Rule of Engagement: We will set aside time together on a regular basis

Keep Their Glass Full

This may sound strange coming from a guy, but I love weddings. I learn something from every single wedding I attend. It's a great chance to watch and talk with people from many different backgrounds and with diverse views on marriage. It's like a living laboratory. Tara and I recently went to a family wedding. The venue was outdoors at a downtown museum. The weather was perfect, and it was great to see extended family that we had not seen in a long time. Between the ceremony and the reception was a cocktail hour with an open bar and appetizers. At one point, the two of us were standing at a table talking when one of the servers came up offering us hors d'oeuvres. She noticed that Tara's drink was almost gone. She looked directly at me and said, "Mhmm, mmmh…You need to keep your lady's glass full if you know what's good for you." We all laughed as she walked away. But I couldn't get those words out of my mind for the rest of the evening.

Her comment had many profound implications. In a literal sense, it could have simply been polite of me to offer Tara a refill before she had to ask. But beyond that, the glass could represent Tara's life or state of mind. Before it would occur to me to keep her glass full, I would have to notice her glass is nearly empty. That would require me to pay sufficient attention to assess the situation and anticipate her needs before they become too great. Her needs clearly go beyond thirst. Knowing my wife better than anyone else on earth should allow me to notice and anticipate her other needs as well.

Keeping her glass full could imply filling an emotional need. If I'm focused, I can detect when Tara is angry, frustrated, uncomfortable, or frightened without her having to tell me. I see that she is getting nervous before she panics or that she's upset before she becomes angry. Putting out a small fire is far easier than extinguishing a major blaze.

Keeping her glass full could even mean meeting a physical need. There are times when I can tell she just needs a hug, and providing that can be far more beneficial than I could ever imagine. Maybe I notice that she's really tired, and I simply jump in to help her on a task she's working on. There have been times when I've come into the house and within minutes take the kids out to play because it's obvious that she needs a break from them.

Noticing a need is a crucial first step, but proactively satisfying it is of even more importance. In our nearly forty years of marriage, there have been times when I have noticed her needs (an emptying glass) but have been too self-absorbed or busy to do anything about it. You get no points for detection if you don't follow up with a solution. It is important to stop, notice the emptying glass, and take the time to refill it.

I'll never know if that waitress was simply suggesting that I get my wife another drink or if she was pointing me toward a far more profound learning. In either case, it was a great reminder.

Speak Their Love Language

A very practical way of keeping your spouse's glass full is to speak their love language. In his book The Five Love Languages[6], Gary Chapman says that each of us has one of five primary love languages: quality time, words of affirmation, acts of service, gifts, and physical touch.

---

6   Chapman, Gary. The Five Love Lanuages, 1992

Each of these represent a distinct manner in which we naturally want to show and be shown love. If you've not read his book, I strongly encourage you to do so. This is a very simple, yet effective step in focusing on each other's needs.

When I was in corporate life, I had a job with global responsibilities. As a result, I traveled extensively on an international basis. A typical trip would span two weeks and three weekends. Traveling to exotic places around the world was very exciting, but it was tough on Tara for me to be gone so much of the time.

Every time I would go to a new place, my first thought was how much I wished that Tara could be with me. With her on my mind, I would consistently set aside some time during the trip to find and buy her something special that I could give to her upon my return. I'm not talking about simply picking up a souvenir at the airport. I would find a local colleague and ask what specifically would represent that particular area in terms of a gift for my wife. I would then determine a way to procure such an item personally to make sure it was perfect for her. This might have been an opal from Australia or inlaid marble art from India.

One time in China, I heard about a very rare variety of loose-leaf tea that could only be bought in the specific region where I was visiting. Before heading to the airport, I found myself riding in an open three-wheeled motorized cart, zipping through crowded streets at breakneck speed to a specific teashop where this tea was sold. I bought a tin of tea from an old Chinese man with only two teeth who didn't speak a word of English. I just knew that Tara would love it.

Fast-forward forty hours, I walk in the front door of my house, jet-lagged and exhausted. My kids swarm me and are giddy with excitement. Tara gives me a big hug to welcome me home. After an hour of catching up, I headed off to take a shower. "Don't take too long," Tara told me. "I've made a nice dinner for you."

Once I emerged from the shower, more tired now than ever, I dug through my bag to grab the gift-wrapped tin of tea. I couldn't wait to give it to her and tell her the story behind it. I took it downstairs and saw that everyone was already seated at the table waiting for me. I sat down, then handed Tara the tea, excited to see her reaction. She was appreciative, but set it on the side table and said, "Let's eat." I was disappointed at her lack of reaction, but I could barely keep my eyes open since my brain was off by ten hours. I really enjoyed eating with the family again but found it hard to eat too much in my jet-lagged state. Once dinner was over, I retired to the living room and promptly fell asleep in front of the television.

This story played out numerous times over the course of about six years. It wasn't until we read the *Love Languages* that we discovered that my primary love language was "gifts" and hers was "acts of service." I'll never forget the conversation that ensued. "You mean all those things that you brought back for me was your way of expressing love? I just assumed you grabbed something you saw that you thought was interesting," Tara stated. I affirmed that was exactly my intent and told her some of the more interesting stories of the effort I had extended to get some of the gifts. She had no idea. She actually began to weep a bit.

Then it hit me. "Wait a second, those big meals you made for me when I got home, that was your expression of love?" Of course it was. I had no idea of the time and effort she had put into the preparation of those special meals. Being exhausted and having eaten at fancy restaurants for two straight weeks led me to underappreciate what she was offering. But in that moment, I realized it was never about the food—it was about her effort in preparing something special for me to enjoy.

Until we understood this concept, we assumed that we both expressed love in the same manner. Knowing your partner's love language and speaking it are very strong expressions of selflessness and consideration. I continued to buy gifts, and Tara continued to make great meals, but we never took them for granted again.

When you speak your partner's love language, you are showing that you are willing to make an effort to put their interests first. The first time I went to France, my coworkers warned me that the French can be quite snobbish if you don't speak their language. While I've never been fluent in any language (including English, according to some of my high school teachers), I made an effort to speak a few key phrases in French while at hotels or in restaurants. I was amazed at the change of attitude I saw once I extended this effort. While I feared I would be ridiculed for my lack of linguistics, the exact opposite occurred. The French hospitality staff appreciated me making the effort and went to considerable ends to assist me in my requests. The same is true in your marriage. Your efforts will show intent and serve as an expression of true love.

Be Intentional

There are a lot of elements involved in keeping the spark alive within your marriage. Committing to a stronger marriage involves an ongoing effort and must supersede day-to-day feelings. Shocking marriages hold on to their commitments of continuous growth even during low seasons. They recognize low seasons are only temporary, and better days lie just around the corner. I've heard economy experts say that the best time to invest in the stock market is during a recession. Prices are low, but they will inevitably rebound. Investments during these times have tremendous rates of return. Marriage is no different. Investing in a night away or in a special date night can convert your blasé feelings into excitement and even passion.

One of the ways we are intentional is in setting annual goals. We go out to dinner to celebrate our anniversary, and one of my favorite parts of the evening is when we reflect on the past year of marriage and proactively plan for the upcoming year. We'll talk about highs and lows and discuss areas where we've grown closer and areas where we've drifted a bit. Even after nearly forty years of marriage, I still make a lot of assumptions about how Tara perceives things (and vice versa). Something that I think went really well, she may have perceived as falling short. Then we'll shift our thinking to the coming year. What is it we would love to accomplish in the next year of marriage? What do we want to change? While the primary focus is specifically on shared goals within our relationship, we also talk about goals that we have as individuals. We express love when we support each other in these pursuits. Dreaming about the future bonds us together. Accomplishing our goals or not is far less important than taking the time to talk together and plan for the future. It's harder to drift apart if you regularly ensure you are headed toward the same future goal.

Rule of Engagement: We will regularly assess our relationship and proactively plan for the future.

Discussion Questions

- Look back at your marriage with your spouse (for the past month, year, five years—whatever is applicable). Describe times when you felt your relational fire was really roaring. What did that look like? What did it feel like? What were some of the specific events/activities that were taking place during that time?
- Look back over the same time period. Describe times when you felt your relational fire was dwindling. What did that look like? How did that feel? What were the situations in your relationship during that time?
- Consider what took place that caused your fire to either grow or diminish.
- What are some tangible warning signs your fire may be fading? What specific actions can you take to stoke it back up?
- What rules of engagement could you create to keep you aware and on track in this area?
- What are your respective love languages (if you are not sure, take a free online test at 5lovelanguages. com to see)? How well do you "speak" your spouse's love language? How could you do this more effectively?
- How well does your spouse speak your love language? Share your thoughts with them.
- Think of one to two goals you would like to pursue over the next year to keep your spark alive.

CHAPTER 8
PHYSICAL INTIMACY

Intimacy in a marriage is comprised of three different, yet related areas: spiritual, emotional and physical. Before a couple can be truly intimate with each other, it is important they have intimacy with God. This happens through getting to know God better through scripture reading, prayer and worship. Emotional intimacy involves providing an atmosphere where each spouse can feel safe and comfortable in their marriage. It's about supporting one another, putting the other's needs first and expressing love in a non-physical manner. Physical intimacy is what many men first think of when they hear the word, as it involves sex. All three aspects of intimacy are critical and should be kept in balance with one another. For the purposes of this book, I will be focusing on physical intimacy. You can learn more about the other forms of intimacy in my book "Beyond the Celebration – The Essential Guide to Creating a Marriage of Mutual Respect, Lasting Love, Joy, Hilarity and Great Sex".

Physical intimacy can be a challenging topic for many couples in a Christian marriage. We are all products of our culture and our upbringing. Some people were raised in homes where sex was openly discussed, and they received extensive advice prior to getting married. Others were raised in homes where the very mention of sex was taboo. They were raised to feel sex was something nasty that should only be performed in order to procreate. Regardless of the specific environment, most people were raised with the idea that sex is an extremely private topic making it sometimes difficult to discuss -even with their spouse.

The internet is filled with sites offering sexual advice for Christian marriages. There is no reason for someone to be ignorant about sex today as they might have been a few generations ago. But even with so much information available, attitudes toward sex vary widely. As a result, what one Christian couple considers as healthy and enticing in terms of sex, may be condemned by another Christian couple as wrong or even sinful. Couples develop a sex life that works for them and label that as normal. When they hear or read of another couple that vary from their norm, it is not uncommon to either envy or sit in judgement of them. Isn't it interesting that we are all operating under the same God-given user's manual, the Bible?

My goal is not to suggest "one right way" to express or enjoy physical intimacy within your marriage. No two people are identical; certainly, no two couples are. That is a beautiful thing. God created sex and intends for married couples to enjoy it and discover what most satisfies them. It is up to each couple to determine what is right and desirable for them. That sounds easy, doesn't it?

Unfortunately, in many marriages spouses may have markedly different sex drives. As a result, physical intimacy often becomes a source of conflict. Frustration that stems from this (either lack of sex or the feeling of having too much sex) may surface in other, unrelated aspects of the relationship. Satisfying both spouses' physical needs can be challenging, but is critical. It will probably require some compromise on both parties. But if you are committed to continually improving your marriage and putting your spouse's needs first, you can find a way to manage this. Rules pertaining to sex should not be ignored. Creating guidelines for physical intimacy allows you to give this area of your marriage proper consideration so that over time, it won't be neglected, and you will both be satisfied.

The Game with No Winners

In the workshops Tara and I have led, numerous men have vented to us about the lack of sex in their marriage. "My wife is always too tired, doesn't feel well, or just isn't in the mood. It's maddening." Many will go on to express they feel completely at their wife's mercy when it comes to their sexual relationship. These husbands may be leaders in other areas, but when it comes to intimacy, they find themselves having to bargain or even plead for sex. When counseling one frustrated husband in this regard I heard, "When we do have sex, it's completely up to her, when, where, and how. I have little say in the matter. But I'm afraid to complain or bring it up in conversation for risk of being cut off completely."

Conversely, women often express concern about the lack of nonsexual attention they get from their husbands. "Why can't my husband just hold me? Why does it always have to lead to sex? I don't mind sex, but that shouldn't be the only time that he will touch me." This inevitably becomes a self-fulfilling prophecy. When he does reach out to put his arm around her, or give her a kiss, she immediately assumes that he is trying to seduce her. Finding this offensive, she gives him the (typically nonverbal) message that she is not interested in sex, which in turn drives him away.

Behaviors such as these don't always fall so cleanly along gender lines. Sometimes it's the wife with the stronger sex drive, and the husband is less interested. While the roles may sometimes be reversed, the tension remains the same. When one spouse rejects their partner's advances long enough, they may eventually quit offering any kind of physical attention at all. These feelings of rejection are detrimental to the relationship. For the purpose of simplicity in this chapter, I will go with the assumption that the man has the stronger drive. Feel free to reverse the roles if applicable.

Is it possible to satisfy the needs of both partners when they're so seemingly different? The answer is yes, but it requires a new mind-set for each person. In this area, more than others, men and women are wired differently. A 1995 study conducted by the Kinsey Institute showed that 54 percent of men thought about sex several times per day. Only 19 percent of women thought about sex even once a day. This study was an average of men and women of all ages. It's probably safe to assume that the numbers are even higher for men in their prime physical years.

Though it may be unintentional, from a relational standpoint, you create the situation in which you're living. Both genders are often guilty of baiting and switching through the transition from dating to marriage. Dating men may buy expensive gifts for their girlfriends. They may be willing to sit and talk for hours.

Strolling down the beach hand in hand? Of course! That is until they actually marry, at which time many of these seductive behaviors quickly dissipate. Likewise, if a couple is sexually active prior to marriage, it is not uncommon for the woman to say or do various things in an effort to "catch" a husband. Once he's on the hook, her personal preferences kick in, and these lures also go away. Every marriage goes through a passionate honeymoon phase where a couple just can't seem to get enough of each other, but this phase doesn't last forever.

Once the honeymoon phase subsides, unhealthy, selfish behaviors may kick in. Many women begin to use sex as a reward for behavior they want to encourage or withhold it as punishment for undesired behavior. "If he buys me flowers, I'll give him sex," or "He's not going to get any tonight based on the comment he made this morning." Over time, the husband adapts to certain patterns. Sex is a strong motivator for men, and they will naturally take the path of least resistance to get it. Even though they know they are being manipulated, they will often play the game to achieve their end goal.

Guys, on the other hand, are always looking for an opening to advance sex. If the wife cozies up next to him on the couch, there's physical contact. "Aha! Here's my chance" is the first thought that comes to his mind. "If I just touch her in the right places in the right sequence, she's sure to want sex. At least that used to work." He spends his emotional energy trying to sell her on the idea of sex, but ultimately, she's the buyer. If she doesn't pull the trigger to close the sale, he gets frustrated and grumpy. She knows this and comes to learn the minimum frequency for which she needs to say yes to keep him from going off the deep end. And the ugly, frustrating game continues.

Changing the Rules

Before we began offering marriage workshops, our pastor led a series on sexuality in marriage. He discussed biblical examples of healthy sexual attitudes as seen in Song of Solomon and the consequences of unhealthy behaviors, such as David and Bathsheba. In the last week of the series, he pointed out that in our modern times, we've developed a warped perspective on sex. He then quoted the following scripture.

> Do not deprive each other of sexual relations, unless you both agree to refrain from sexual intimacy for a limited time so you can give yourselves more completely to prayer. Afterward, you should come together again so that Satan won't be able to tempt you because of your lack of self-control.

> 1 Corinthians 7: 5 NLT

He went on to teach that "Not tonight, I have a headache," or "The kids have been rotten today, I just can't," or "I'm just not in the mood" are not scripturally valid reasons for a partner to say no. He added that if the husband is following the biblical model of marriage, he would be in tune with his wife enough to understand and respect those times when the situation is not ideal for sex. He told us that that in our Christian culture, women may consider their husbands to be head of the household in most areas, but when it comes to having sex, most retain absolute control. He challenged the ladies of our church to not say no without good reason.

It felt like a long walk out of the church that morning with my mind reeling from the sermon. Tara and I had a great marriage, but honestly, sex was the one ongoing issue that led to conflict and hurt feelings. Just as our pastor had described, I felt like this was one area where I was completely subject to her whims, moods, and desires. When she would decline my expressed interest, it would often end in an argument with both of us justifying our perspectives. My fear was this sermon had stirred up the proverbial hornet's nest, so I was determined to avoid the topic.

As we began to drive away from the church, Tara calmly asked me, "What did you think of the sermon?" While this was not an atypical question, I wanted to change the subject as quickly as I could. I couldn't figure out a way to do so without being overly obvious. So, instead of diverting, I reversed the question and asked her, "What did you think of it?" offering no opinion of my own. Tara told me that she had never heard this particular scripture taught before and felt convicted by the message. "Okay," I said cautiously, "so what does that mean for us?" She sat quietly, obviously thinking and praying as I began the drive home. After a few miles, she looked at me and said, "Let's try it." Not wanting to make any stupid assumptions, and looking straight out the windshield at the road, I asked her, "Okay. What exactly do you mean by that?" She told me that for the next thirty days, she wouldn't say no when I initiated sex. I was stunned by this and drove for a couple of miles without saying a word. Finally, I nervously asked what she expected of me in return. Her response was something to the effect of "I don't have any conditions. I would only request that you be sensitive to me and my needs."

Much to Tara's surprise, it took me a few days to initiate sex. I don't know if I was concerned that she wasn't serious about her offer or if the pressure of knowing she'd say yes just flummoxed me in the short term. In any case, it turned out to be a fantastic thirty days for both of us. At the end of the time, we reflected and spoke openly about the experience. Our biggest realization was that we had both been playing unhealthy games in this area. Specific learning included the following:

- *In the past, I requested sex more often than what I really wanted.* At some level, I figured that if I was told no two out of every three times that I requested sex, I would compensate by asking three times more than I wanted it. From my perspective, this improved my overall odds of getting a yes with sufficient frequency. From Tara's perspective, I asked all the time, even in ridiculous situations. Saying no to any given request was not a big deal. She knew I'd ask again soon.

- *The actual frequency of sex remained unchanged from previous months.* Tara was convinced that this month would be a throwback to early marriage. To her surprise, the actual frequency did not change much, but the tension and conflict generated from my constant nagging went away.

- *Not having to "work for it" changed my attitude toward Tara.* I found myself being more attentive to her non-sexual needs. I wasn't worried about getting worked up now and being frustrated later. As a result, I didn't hesitate to cuddle on the couch or hold her hand. My motivation for physical contact changed from trying to "get her in the mood" to simply expressing affection. I knew that if I wanted intimacy, she would agree. From her perspective, the amount of nonsexual touch she craved increased dramatically. Knowing sex was available at any time made me more sensitive to her current mood and situation. If I could tell she was stressed-out or very tired, I saw no reason to ask; it could wait for a better moment. This was affirming for her and became very natural to me.

- *Our petty arguments all but came to an end.* We both noticed there was less tension in our relationship. I realized I had been harboring resentment toward Tara for rejecting my advances. This might have been expressed as complaints about unrelated things, like a mess in the house or the kid's behavior. But it was actually me lashing out at her for rejecting my advances. From Tara's perspective, it seemed I would start complaining the moment I came into the house, making her resentful and less likely to agree to sex. The cycle would continue until Tara would agree to have "pity sex," an act that I despised but accepted anyway. During this rejection-free month, I no longer had the feelings of frustration that would start our downward spiral, which eliminated our daily arguments.

- *The microwave/crock pot analogy is misleading.* You've probably heard the analogy that men are like microwave ovens, ready for sex at a moment's notice, and that women are like Crock-Pots that heat up slowly. In the past I took that to mean if I wanted to have sex in the evening, I needed to work for it all day long. I would rub Tara's shoulders in the morning before I'd leave for work. I would make a special effort to call her a few times during the day and walk in the door with nothing but compliments coming from my mouth. In my mind, I had performed all of the necessary steps to guarantee sex once it came time for bed. Tara's perspective was different. From the first shoulder rub in the morning, she would think, "I know what he's up to." When she answered my phone calls, in her mind she would say, "He only calls when he wants sex." By the time I arrived home with my compliments, she had decided, "I know exactly what you want, and that's just not going to happen." All of my efforts to express affection made her feel manipulated, making the thought of having sex almost repulsive. Removing rejection allowed me to focus on her needs out of love rather than working to earn sex, allowing her to freely receive my affection without fearing a hidden agenda. When I request sex, she's willing, not because of what I've done the last four hours, but rather because of how I've treated her over the course of days or even weeks.

After thirty days neither wanted to go back to our old ways. What started as an experiment has become a way of life for us. Sex is not a right to be demanded or a treat to be begged for but a beautiful expression of love and intimacy to be enjoyed by both of us. Since that time, I have recommended this thirty-day challenge to other couples that have expressed similar frustrations in their own marriages. Feedback from them afterwards in terms of their experience was very similar to what we enjoyed.

Based on our learning and adjusted lifestyle, we created the following two rules to help keep us on track. Reminding ourselves of these help us from sliding back into the issues we experienced before.

Rule of Engagement: Make "yes" the default answer when my partner asks for sex.

Rule of Engagement: Never use sex as a tool or associate it with power.

Don't be Afraid to Schedule Sex

The thought of scheduling sex may sound appalling to you. You may think that sex should be organic and happen naturally – an outpouring of love expressed between you and your spouse. There's nothing wrong with that thinking, except it tends to conflict with real life and the culture that you live in. Sex is important in a marriage. You put important things on your calendar, so scheduling sex should be no different. This takes conversation and agreement, but once you are aligned, it will greatly simplify life for the both of you.

Say for example that you agree that you'd like to schedule sex twice a week. You consider other commitments that exist and agree to plan for Tuesday nights and Saturday mornings. Just as you do with other calendar events, you mentally prepare for these times. There's not negotiating or pleading, you both know it's going to happen then.

This can be a great tool for couples with differing sex drives. For the partner with the lesser drive, it takes away the need to make a decision or to concede to sex. For the partner with the stronger drive, it gives them something to look forward to.

Just as with any calendar event, these times can be cancelled for sickness or an unexpected event that takes precedence. The goal is to have these set as scheduled times that the both of you honor whenever possible. Scheduled sex should not be the only sex that you have. You still want to allow for spontaneity, special occasions or other times when the moment is right. Scheduling sex just gives it a priority in your marriage which should be honored just as other commitments are.

The Beauty of Long-Term Commitment

I've heard some single people say that they can't imagine only sleeping with one person for the rest of their lives—the boredom would be overwhelming and intolerable. These people are not looking for or following God's design for marriage, as the Bible clearly speaks of man and woman becoming one flesh and remaining together for life. Physical oneness through sexual intimacy is a part of the one flesh idea, but the concept doesn't stop there. As a couple lives together in a covenant relationship, their two lives become one in many ways. Beyond physical intimacy, they begin to share convictions, beliefs, and even life goals. They share each other's joys and feel each other's pain. These shared traits follow right into the bedroom.

I find tremendous beauty in the fact that I know what pleases my wife and she knows what I most enjoy. In fact, we know things about each other that no one else on earth could possibly know, and because of that, our relationship is special. Many of these preferences and dislikes were not learned overnight but over many years of being together. In fact, we're still learning! The techniques we enjoyed as twenty-something newlyweds are not necessarily the same ones we most appreciate now, nearly forty years later. Had we not evolved with each other over time, our marriage would not be where it is now.

One of the greatest aspects of long-term marriage is the ability to be completely vulnerable. There is no need to put up a façade or try to pretend to be something you're not. You can share a level of honesty and openness that is not experienced in any other relationship. Unconditional love takes away fear and insecurity. Intimacy may change in form over time, but it should continue to grow in depth.

The Challenges of Long-Term Commitment

Marriages evolve over time. Selfishness can creep into a relationship. In the early stages of marriage, it is easy to focus on your partner's needs rather than your own. As you first discover the likes and preferences of your spouse, you are excited to explore and see what else you might do to please them. Eventually, the energy once focused on your spouse can shift to your personal needs and desires. Sex becomes more about your personal expectations rather than meeting the needs of your partner. As selfishness increases, intimacy decreases.

It saddens me when I hear long-married couples talk about boredom in the bedroom. My question back to them is always, "Well, whose fault is that?" Being married for a long time to the same person should lead to comfort, but not to monotony. Comfort is a wonderful thing, but when carried to an extreme can become routine and complacency sets in. It's easy to lie in bed and follow a well-established pattern leading up to sex. Many couples could probably plot out their typical sex routine in a simple step-by-step format. Imagine you've fallen into the habit of making love every Saturday morning. You wake up in the same bed at the same time. You initiate sex in the customary manner. Your partner responds exactly as you expect them to, and so on and so forth. This goes on for months, maybe even years. It's just what you do. How do you spell boredom? R-o-u-t-i-n-e. There's nothing inherently wrong with this scenario. It's predictable and easy. It doesn't require a lot of thought, imagination, or effort and can be both comfortable and satisfying. While this might lead to short-term physical satisfaction, it certainly leaves the mental aspect lacking. Over time, boredom will reduce frequency until sex becomes merely an infrequent, physical release. Don't let routine sex be your only encounters. Albert Einstein is quoted as saying, "The definition of insanity is doing the same thing over and over again and expecting different results." This is as true in the bedroom as it is in any other aspect of life.

Mixing things up doesn't have to be excessively complicated. Changing any small part of the routine can make a big difference and break you out of a habit. Choose a different position, day of the week, time of day, or even room of the house. Changing a routine even slightly can free up your mind to be more in the moment with your spouse.

Go somewhere overnight without the kids from time to time. Sex in a new venue can change everything. Once your long-standing patterns are interrupted, you will find yourselves reinventing the entire process. It takes time and effort to step outside your normal routine, but you will find that it is worth it.

Keeping It Fresh

It takes intentionality to stay focused on your spouse's needs over time. One of the greatest ways to keep your love life energized over time is to openly discuss sex with your spouse. This sounds so obvious, but many couples struggle with having conversations about sex. They may not be inhibited in the bedroom, but the thought of talking about likes, dislikes, fantasies and techniques falls out of their comfort zone. It is important to be open about your feelings and your desires with your spouse. Here are some thoughts to make this easier for you.

- Have discussions during non-intimate times.
    - o Trying to start a conversation during sex can be distracting and annoying. Have it at a private time when you won't be interrupted. Talk about past experiences as well as desired future ones.
- Be objective and listen actively.
- Ask open-ended questions that encourage discussion.
    - o Instead of asking "Are you happy with our sex life?" ask "From your perspective, what could we do to improve our sex life?" The second question gives permission to voice an opinion that doesn't have to be justified or supported with facts. No matter how good a relationship is, there's always room for improvement.
    - o Encourage them to dream or fantasize about what they would love to experience with you in a sexual manner.
- Use *we* and *our* to show that you are interested in improving as a couple.
    - o "How could we make our sex life more interesting?" is a great question.
    - o Contrast this with "How could I be a better lover for you?" While this may seem like a selfless question, it puts tremendous pressure on the partner being asked to answer honestly without hurting feelings.
- Avoid judgment
    - o Reacting negatively to a thought or suggestion that your partner raises could prevent them from suggesting anything new in the future.

- Communication leads to understanding, which is a starting point to improving intimacy.

Rule of Engagement: We will make efforts to keep sex fresh and fight routine and boredom

Summary

Physical intimacy (sex) is an important aspect of marriage. It bonds a couple together in a way that can't be accomplished otherwise. Issues surrounding sex are common in marriage. The key is to be open and honest with your spouse in terms of discussing your preferences and your opinions. The Bible states that we are to give our bodies to our spouse, so it is important to not be selfish in this regard. Don't use sex as a tool or as a reward, and don't allow sex to be your only form of intimacy. Be careful not to get into a long-term, sexual rut. Keep it fresh and exciting. You can have a great sex life in your marriage, but it takes effort and intentionality.

Discussion Questions

- On a scale of one to ten, with one being "I never want to talk about sex" and ten being "I can talk about anything," how comfortable are you in terms of discussing sex with your spouse? If your score is low, what could help you be more comfortable?
- Individually, list the top three sexual experiences you have had as a married couple. Come together and discuss your lists. How similar or different are your lists? What specifically makes them different? How does this translate into what each of you most desire from sex?
- How aligned are you in terms of frequency and patterns for your sex life? Does one of you have greater control over your sex life, or is it shared equally?
- Would you say you are more spontaneous or routine in your sex life? Do you desire more spontaneity or more routine? Why?
- Plan a special night for sex. It might be at a hotel or just at home but make it a point to vary this from your typical encounter. Think about your answers from the earlier question: what could you do to make this night a top three experience from your spouse's perspective?

CHAPTER 9
MODELING YOUR MARRIAGE

Your marriage is on public display for your kids, your families, your friends, your coworkers, and your neighbors. Some of those audiences may care more about what they see than others, but don't think for a minute that people aren't noticing how you and your spouse interact.

People are not just observing your relationship; they are judging it as well. It may not be intentional, but couples compare their marriage to other marriages all the time. They watch and take note of how you show love, communicate, make decisions, disagree, even raise your kids. In some instances, comparisons can help a couple to feel better about their own marriage. "Well, at least we don't fight like the Watsons." Other times, they use comparisons to complain to their spouse, "Why don't you ever hold my hand in public like Michelle's husband does?" When people see and evaluate a shocking marriage, they may still see flawed humans but they also see a relationship they would like to model.

Marriage is a Powerful Testimony of Your Faith

God didn't intend for His design of marriage to be shocking. He intended for it to be the standard. But a marriage that reflects His will stands out in our fallen world.

Marriage is a covenant relationship that reflects Christ's love for the church. Ephesians 5:25 says, "Husbands, love your wives, just as Christ loved the church, and gave himself up for her." We should model this type of sacrificial love in our marriages. Our first love must be God, but our second love must be for our spouse. Only then can we truly model the gospel to a watching world.

Your marriage can be a powerful witness to those who are not believers. One of the realities of being a Christian is that our unbelieving family and friends are watching to see if our commitment to follow Jesus affects how we live. If they perceive that our lives are no different from theirs, it may help justify their choice of unbelief.

Many people get married in a church and recite traditional vows. Even if they wed outside of the church, most will still use a minister of some sort. But that is where the similarity between the marriages of believers and nonbelievers ends. Whereas for some, vows are just "beautiful words," as Christians we are making a covenant vow before God that we will honor, cherish, love, and support our spouse "until death do us part." Christian marriages should be shocking because we are determined to live this out over the course of our lives and our marriages. When the world sees marital discord or divorce in the Christian community, it puts us on an equal playing field. And that's not where we're called to be. We should have marriages that are visibly different from those that don't have Jesus Christ in their lives. Our marriages should be a living testimony of the power of the Holy Spirit, who changes us individually and as a couple. This is evidenced through our sacrificial love and humility, when we admit our wrongs and ask for forgiveness, and when we have joy in the midst of sorrow. People who don't know Jesus should look at us and think, "I want what they've got." And when they ask us why our marriages are different; we should be prepared with an answer (1 Peter 3:15).

Using your marriage as a Christian witness is not about sugarcoating your lives and making sure that you look happy all of the time. It's about being genuine and letting the love of God shine through you. When Tara and I have conducted marriage workshops, we solicit feedback from our participants at the end. The most common theme we've heard is how much couples enjoyed our transparency and our authenticity. This always struck me as odd because to us that is our normal way of living. When we're with friends or in a small group setting, we strive to be genuine with what is going on in our lives. Why is that so rare? So many Christian couples put on a façade that everything in their world is nearly perfect. The reality is none of us lives a sinless life, and nobody has a perfect marriage. Yet when around church friends, that is often how we portray our lives.

As an elder at our church, it would grieve me when I would learn that a couple in our congregation was seeking a divorce. Usually, by the time I would have a chance to talk with them, they had made up their minds, and it was too late to salvage the relationship. When I would talk with their friends or their small group leaders to see if they had seen this coming, I would hear that they were as surprised as I was to hear the news. People living life with the couple were unaware of the problems that lurked behind closed doors. I wonder how many times these couples would argue all the way to church or to their small group meeting, only to put on a smile once they arrived, indicating they had no need for prayer or counsel. This is not how we are called to live. Imagine if couples embraced the freedom they have as believers and opened up to the people who were closest to them. Perhaps they could have received help before issues got out of hand. Every relationship has problems. We need to develop Christian community with trusted friends who can guide us through the rough patches and confirm that we are not alone.

Modeling Marriage for Your Kids

"Every father should remember that one day his son will follow his example instead of his advice" (Charles F Kettering)[7]. It's important that you choose to create a positive model for your kids. No one will be more impacted by your marriage than the young people watching it every day. You might be able to hide your issues from friends and neighbors, but your kids see you in all situations. They will see your marriage for what it is, warts-and-all. Having a marriage built on a solid foundation can provide your children with tremendous security. A shocking marriage is one of the greatest gifts you can give them.

We should not hide the hard parts of marriage from our kids. Pretending that there are never disagreements is not honest, and it deprives them of the opportunity to learn from watching a conflict be effectively resolved. If

---

7   azquotes.com/quote/597271

you have implemented rules of engagement for conflict, you don't need to be afraid of arguing in front of your children. You'll not be shouting, name-calling, or belittling your spouse. While your arguments may be intense at times, your children will see how you ultimately get to a good solution and realize marriage can be a safe place to disagree. While it may not be your direct intent, this type of positive modeling will teach them how to effectively deal with conflict in their own lives.

Watching how you cope with tough times is another opportunity for learning. Whether you're grieving the loss of a loved one or in a season of financial uncertainty, kids who see their parents rely on each other and on God will gain a sense of peace and security. Letting your kids see that you are human and struggle on occasion is not a bad thing. In fact, allowing them to see you dealing with such struggles in a positive manner is invaluable. It's okay if children walk in and find their parents arguing. But it's fantastic if they walk in and see their parents praying together. Don't underestimate the power of their observation and the long-term impact it will have on their lives.

Helping your children understand the unique relationship that you have with your spouse is of critical importance. I am the father of three sons and have been (or am going through) the teen years with each of them. Testosterone-filled boys will naturally become aggressive and assert themselves in an attempt to establish boundaries and to understand their true role in the family. This can lead to outbursts, arguments, raised voices and even veiled threats. I distinctly remember a time when my oldest son got into an argument with his mother. It started out like most disputes but began to increase in terms of its intensity. I stood nearby watching to see where it was headed. At one point he got so angry that he took both of his hands and physically pushed his mom. At that point I grabbed him by his shirt, pulled him away and got right in his face. "That is my wife!" I said sternly. "I will not allow you or any other man to get physical with her or disrespect her like that." At that moment, I was no longer just Dad. I was Mom's husband and was protecting her as such. Truth be told, that was such an effective technique that I used it for each of his younger brothers when similar situations arose. Years later, my two older sons each told me what an impactful moment that was for them, and it gave them a powerful lesson on how to respect their own wives.

Another important thing we can model for our children is the way we show physical affection to our spouse. Too often, we're more willing to argue than to kiss in front of our children. God forbid they realize we're in love. Physical affection, like all other areas in our marriage, is one where we are modeling behaviors that our kids will one day mimic.

Our culture bombards us with sexual messages in every area except for marriage. While young singles in movies and television are always on the prowl for sex, married couples are often depicted as bored, frustrated, or oblivious. Even today, young adults feel their parents only had sex to procreate. With the exception of "the talk" where we explain the mechanics of making babies, we don't talk about sex as an expression of love, with our kids. We don't flirt with our spouses in front of them. What is the not so subtle message being drilled into their heads? Get plenty while you're single because there's no sex after marriage.

As a couple, we've always been very open about sex around our kids. Not in a graphic or exhibitionist manner, but our children know that we are sexually active with each other. Our older married sons seem to now respect and appreciate that we were open about that part of our relationship. But as you can imagine, it still makes our teens quite uncomfortable.

The importance of letting children see the sexual chemistry between their parents is one of the most surprising things that couples hear from us during our workshops. It's not something most of them experienced growing up, so it's not something they've considered sharing with their own children. Most of them understand the logical reasoning, but many struggle with actually showing affection. Once we remind them that their children are seeing passion in almost every other setting, they typically agree as to its importance.

A short time after one of our workshops, a woman stopped me in the parking lot after church. She told me that during the week her daughter was helping her to fold laundry. Her daughter picked up some scanty panties and asked, "Who's are these?" She calmly reached over, grabbed the underwear and replied, "Those are mine, and your father loves when I wear them!" She went on to tell me that prior to the workshop, she would have been terribly embarrassed, grabbed the panties and told her daughter to not worry about it. She was so proud of her newfound reaction.

Rule of Engagement: We will strive to be transparent with our marriage in front of our children so that they can see a shocking marriage modeled for their own lives

If you don't think modeling is effective, let me give you a brief example. A few years ago, I came home from work, set my stuff on the table, and walked behind my wife as she was working at the stove. Without think-ing twice, I patted her on the bottom and said, "Hey, babe." (my usual greeting upon arriving home). But this particular time, she unexpectedly turned to me and said, "That's where he got it!" Then she burst out laughing. Unbeknownst to me, she had gotten a call from school that day. Our then-eight-year-old son had walked behind his teacher while she was writing on the board and done the same thing to her. The school was appalled. In an odd way, I was quite proud.

Representing Our Spouse to Others

Our words can either enhance our relationships or tear them down. We need to think carefully not only about what we say *to* our spouses but also what we say *about* them to others.

> Kind words are like honey – sweet to the soul and healthy for the body.
>
> Proverbs 16:24 NLT

> The tongue is a small thing that makes grand speeches. But a tiny spark can set a great forest of fire. And among all the parts of the body, the tongue is a flame of fire. It is a whole world of wickedness corrupting your entire body. It can set your whole life on fire, for it is set on fire by hell itself.
>
> James 3:5–6 NLT

I remember as a kid I had an uncle who delighted in telling stories about my aunt at holiday dinners.

While they were intended to be humorous, they typically involved some mistake or misstep she had made since our last gathering. As he would begin each story, she would plead with him not to share it, which just seemed to increase his eagerness to tell the tale. Even though I was young at the time, I recall the discomfort I felt watching my aunt blush and attempt to hide her embarrassment.

My uncle was not alone in this behavior. I've seen many people use their spouse as fodder for humorous stories. I've heard many women emasculate their husbands when they publicly ridicule their inability to repair things or get things done around the house. Sadly, these conversations often become a bit of a competition within the group. It's not uncommon after hearing one such story to hear another person try to top the first one, "You think that's bad? My wife is so dumb that she..." And so it goes, with each person trying to outdo the spouse described before. Over time, when we speak of our spouse in a demeaning manner, we begin to believe our own words. Even when meant as humor, our disrespect begins to build. The line between humor and resentment can be very thin.

Rule of Engagement: We will not speak negatively of our spouse in front of others, even in jest

The flip side to this rule is that I will lift up my spouse when referring to them with others. If you do this, you will be amazed how other people treat your spouse. If you show a high degree of respect, others will follow suit.

Mentor and Be Mentored

My parents were my first marriage role models. My father was a tremendous husband for the entire seventy plus years of his marriage. I never doubted my dad loved my mom because he demonstrated his love in ways I could easily see. The following serve as examples of how I saw love demonstrated as I grew up.

- Every year in June a single rose would appear in a bud vase. This was not to celebrate their wedding anniversary, but the anniversary of their first date. Not a year went by without seeing that rose on the table. My mom would practically glow every time it would appear. When my mom passed away a couple of years ago, Dad had seventy-three roses placed on her casket as a tribute to their incredible marriage.
- We lived in a farmhouse with a detached, unheated garage. My mom taught school in a neighboring town and had to leave for work quite early in the mornings, often in the dark and cold of winter. Dad would go outside, shovel snow, get to the car, and have it running and warm before she needed to leave. Mom never climbed into an icy car and never had to walk through snow to leave for work.
- Dad was a constant flirt. I distinctly remember Mom standing at the stove cooking dinner. He couldn't walk by without "goosing" her. She would feign shock and disgust, but I would always notice the resulting smile from the attention he had paid her.

My father was not the perfect husband. I'm sure there were times when my mom was frustrated or aggravated with something he had done. But honestly, I don't remember those instances. What I do remember is what he imprinted on my mind: a wife is a person to hold in the highest regards and to love and respect above anyone else.

Mom always told people that one of her greatest charges in life was to raise four great future husbands. From an early age, she taught us how to cook and clean and always be respectful of women. She warned us that if we left our clothes on the floor, our future wives would be very frustrated. There is no doubt in my mind that this pattern of modeling and intentional teaching is the reason that my brothers and I are all in such great marriages.

You may have come from a broken or dysfunctional home. Or you may have been the product of a loving but single parent. The behaviors you saw modeled may not be anything that you want to replicate. You don't have to fall into the patterns you were raised with. You can model your marriage after other couples, or even after the teachings of Jesus. Showing unconditional love, freely showing grace and forgiveness, using kind and encouraging words are all ways you can build a shocking marriage for yourselves.

Christian discipleship is the process of having believers who are more mature in the faith work with those who are newer in the faith to become more like Jesus over time. Many churches offer training in this area or have whole programs dedicated to this idea. Scripture shows us that the apostle Paul had a relationship with Timothy, a younger believer whom he mentored. At the same time, he had a relationship with Barnabas, a believer more mature in his faith. No matter where we are in our walk, I think we are called to have the same type of relationships. Someone further along than we are who can help us as we enter new situations, and someone newer in the faith that we ourselves can guide.

While this is a proven model for Christian living, I think it can be expanded to include a focus on marriage. Imagine if every couple had a trusted mentor-couple whom they could be completely transparent with—a relationship with no judgment or condemnation. An environment where any question could be asked and answered with no embarrassment. Where topics could range from sex to finance to relations with in-laws.

In many ways we keep our marriages so private that every couple is forced to recreate the proverbial wheel. Seeking out a mentor-couple could save considerable time and emotional energy. Don't know what to do when your two-year old is throwing a tantrum? You want to discipline, but your husband wants to ignore. There are couples that have been through that and can offer guidance. Feeling like your sex life is in a state of rapid decline? You're not the first to experience it. There are couples that have worked through the same experience and are better off for it.

Rule of Engagement: We will be open to learning behaviors and practices from other couples that will benefit us in our own marriage

But as you are mentored, you should consider finding a younger couple that can benefit from your marriage experience. Finding an older couple that can help you through life is wonderful. Finding a younger couple that you can help is fantastic too.

Summary

As believers your marriage is a testimony to your family, your friends and the outside world. Just as we are called to be in the world and not of the world, our marriages should be and look different from those outside of the faith. Be intentional about the model you are providing for your children – they will likely imitate the behaviors they witness in their own marriages one day.

Learn from couples that are farther along (both literally and spiritually) in their marriages. But also, mentor couples that are newer in their marriages and faith. Continue to study scripture to better understand and reflect the type of marriage that God intends for you to have.

Discussion Questions

- What kind of role model for marriage did you have growing up? How similar/dissimilar is this to your spouse's experience? What behaviors you saw modeled do you want to incorporate into your marriage? What behaviors do you want to avoid?
- What kind of model are you providing to your kids? What would their reaction be if they saw you in an argument? What if they saw you kissing?
- Can you think of an older couple that has a shocking marriage? Are there things you can learn from watching them?
- What does your marriage say to a watching world? Do they see the gospel being modeled through your relationship? How could you put more emphasis on this?
- If Christ loved the Church and gave himself up for her, what does it look like give yourself up for your spouse?

CHAPTER 10
EFFECTIVE COMMUNICATION

A good man brings good things out of the good stored up in his heart, and an evil man brings evil things out of the evil stored up in his heart. For the mouth speaks what the heart is full of.

Luke 6:45 NIV

Effective communication is the last chapter of this book, for a reason. Certainly not because it's the least important. Quite the contrary. Lack of communication is a considerable challenge for most couples and one of the primary concerns that couples in distress complain about. Effective communication consists of multiple, distinct parts, what is said, how it is said, and how it is received.

The Power of Your Words

We've discussed throughout this book how to enhance various aspects of your marriage. Hopefully by now your heart is full of love and respect for your spouse. When that is the case, the words that you speak will reflect those feelings. You should never have to search for "something nice to say." Such sentiments will come naturally when your heart is right. Conversely, before you speak out critically against your spouse, you should first look to your own heart to understand your motivations. If you are struggling with this, take it to the Lord in prayer. Use the power of the Holy Spirit to soften or even change your heart.

Rule of Engagement: I will search my heart before I say something unkind

This can be a tough rule to follow, especially after a bad day or in the heat of conflict. But it is critical to understand how destructive our words can be. Consider the following passage.

When we put bits into the mouths of horses to make them obey us, we can turn the whole animal. Or take ships as an example. Although they are so large and are driven by strong winds, they are steered by a very small rudder wherever the pilot wants to go. Likewise, the tongue is a small part of the body, but it makes great boasts. Consider what a great forest is set on fire by a small spark. The tongue also is a fire, a world of evil among the parts of the body. It corrupts the whole body, sets the whole course of one's life on fire, and is itself set on fire by hell. All kinds of animals, birds, reptiles and sea creatures are being tamed and have been tamed by mankind, but no human being can tame the tongue. It is a restless evil, full of deadly poison. With the tongue we praise our Lord and Father, and with it we curse human beings, who have been made in God's likeness. Out of the same mouth come praise and cursing. My brothers and sisters, this should not be. Can both fresh water and salt-water flow from the same spring? My brothers and sisters, can a fig tree bear olives, or a grapevine bear figs? Neither can a salt spring produce fresh water.

James 3:3–12 NIV

Obviously, this is not a new challenge unique to our culture. Since the fall of man, our words have had the power to tear one another down. It's great, and important, to apologize if we stumble and use words we regret. It is so much better to avoid saying harsh words to begin with. While forgiveness can and should occur, words cannot be unheard.

Expectations of Communication

I'll never forget the first time I led a marriage study. I was the leader of a church small group that consisted of eight couples ranging in age from their thirties to their fifties. Each group was allowed to choose the topic of the study they wanted to pursue, be it a book of the Bible or a relevant topical study. Our group decided they wanted to do a study on making marriages stronger. At the time, I didn't consider myself an expert in this area, but I figured Tara and I could facilitate a discussion on this topic as well as any other we had done. I went to the Christian Bookstore and selected a book, purchased study guides for everyone, and began the study the following week. We were in our fourth session when we hit the lesson on communication. While we normally just covered the discussion questions as a group, on this particular evening, I kept the men in one room, and Tara took the women in another. We asked each group to identify the biggest issues they faced in terms of communication within their marriage. The intent was to spend about fifteen minutes doing this, then come back together to share the results. The men were done in the allotted fifteen minutes and relocated to the food table. At that point, it was obvious the women were really engaged in animated conversation, so I let them go longer. After about forty-five minutes, the women finished their discussion, and we brought the groups back together to share the lists.

For the most part, the husbands did not see lack of communication as a problem, they focused more on clarity. Their list stated they wanted their wives to communicate more clearly, more specifically, and at more appropriate times (e.g., not in the middle of a televised football game).

The women on the other hand, had a much more exhaustive list, including their desire for more-frequent higher-quality communication. They wanted their husbands to be better listeners and be more willing to share their feelings. None of this was a surprise to the husbands; most had heard these requests before. Then the women shared a final item that left the men speechless. "Finally, we expect you to know what we want or need without us having to tell you." After a long and awkward silence, one of the husbands began to laugh nervously, which caused all the other men in the group to join in. They thought the wives were striving to be humorous with such an outrageous request. After a few minutes of laughter and sarcastic commentary, the men looked up to notice that the women were not laughing; in fact, they weren't even smiling. The wives saw no humor in this, as they had meant their comment quite literally. The biggest shock for me was that my wife was right there with them, looking just as offended as the other ladies!

The conversation became quite animated. The women would not back down. The men saw this request as absurd. Here I was trying to lead a marriage enrichment study, and couples were headed home barely speaking to one another.

After that evening, Tara and I had our own conversation about this controversial request. While she agreed with the point the women were making, she could also appreciate how that put men in a no-win situation. We decided that being attentive could allow a spouse to anticipate preferences and moods, but no one should be held accountable for being a mind reader. Effective communication starts with vocalization, not telepathy. This became our first rule of engagement outside of conflict.

Rule of Engagement: I will not expect my spouse to know my wants and needs if I don't communicate them

This rule eliminated much of the frustration and anger under the surface just waiting to erupt. If Tara was having a tough day, when I arrived home, she would tell me, "I need a break. Do something with the kids." Upon hearing that, I was happy to jump in and honor her request. Hearing her request allowed me to reprioritize my mental to-do list and not just jump into a task that I had been planning without considering her needs. This provided her with the break she deserved but also kept her from resenting me because I didn't offer her assistance without being asked.

As marriages mature, couples should become more in tune with their partner's needs. But it takes intentionality and effort. It's a beautiful thing when you can anticipate and satisfy your spouse's desires without being asked. But don't let resentment set in if you don't ask, and they don't respond.

When Communication Isn't...

I still remember my freshman communications class in college. The bulk of the class taught students how to make a variety of presentations and speeches. But there was one early lecture that focused on the theory of communication. The professor provided a diagram showing that there was always a source of communication and there was a target. There may be a variety of ways the message can be transmitted, but there is always a sender and a receiver. Sometimes there is a barrier between the two that can disrupt or distort the communication. We've all been the victim of a bad cell phone connection. The bottom line; a message sent but not received is not communication.

During the first session of our marriage workshops, we ask couples to share their top marriage frustrations. While men's answers will vary from man to man and from group to group, women almost always say they want their husbands to communicate more. You can tell from the look on the men's faces this is not the first time they've heard this, but they are not sure what to do about it.

It's no secret that men and women communicate differently. Women are typically much better multitaskers than men. My mom and my wife shared this interesting skill. They were both able to do dishes, make grocery lists, follow a television show on in the background, and listen to a story I was telling at the same time. It was not uncommon for me to lose my own train of thought with all the distraction around me. But if I were to ever ask either of them what I'd been saying, they could recall my last ten sentences almost verbatim. That has always been incomprehensible to me.

Men tend to be very focused on one item at a time. I can't tell you how many times I've been surprised to learn we were meeting some couple for dinner when I was planning on a simple evening at home. As hard as I would try, I could not recall ever hearing of such a plan or agreeing to such a commitment. Even though Tara insisted "I told you," if I was mentally engaged in another activity when Tara came in and said something, it was a message sent but not received. Just as my college professor would say, "That is not communication."

Distinguishing the Importance of the Message

In our marriage, we have learned communication naturally falls into different degrees of importance ranging from casual to critical. Each of these is treated with a different level of attention and interaction. In the most casual conversations, we might both find ourselves focused on something different (typically our smartphones). One or the other of us might stumble across something on Facebook and make an audible comment such as "Huh, that's interesting . . ." If the other hears that and is at a point to listen, they might respond, and a conversation will happen. On the other hand, if the other is deeply engrossed in their own train of thought, the comment goes unacknowledged, and that is okay as well. There are no expectations in this regard, so there are no disappointments.

If communication is of a more important nature, we become more intentional about it. We'll start by making sure we have the other person's attention. "Do you have a minute? I want to talk to you about_____."

This is a request, and it gives the other an opportunity to either agree to the conversation at that moment or to politely defer to a later time. Out of respect, we will usually make every effort right then to engage, but sometimes we are in the middle of something and will not be able to devote the attention an important conversation deserves at that moment.

However, when one of us expresses a critical need for conversation, the other agrees to drop what they are doing and give the moment their highest priority and undivided attention. This could mean stopping a conversation with the kids or getting off the phone right away. These times are rare, and we reserve them for situations that really demand immediate, focused attention.

You may think that all of this sounds overly rigid and structured. We have not put each of these specific categories into rules of engagement. In fact, prior to this writing, we've never openly discussed that this is what we do. This is really more of an observation of what we do, recognizing what works for us. Our overarching rule is actually quite simple.

Rule of Engagement: We will give effective communication high priority in our marriage

My examples above merely show what living out that rule looks like in our relationship. There are other communication tips and tricks that we have picked up over the course of our marriage. Some of these naturally developed over time, and others we learned from married couples that we have tremendous respect for and modeled after.

Problem-Solving vs. Listening

An issue that commonly surfaces in marriages is the misunderstanding of the purpose of some conversations. While no gender stereotypes are absolute, they often represent a majority of the population. One of these stereotypes surrounds the area of problem-solving. Most men are wired to solve problems. Women, on the other hand, often like to process their challenges by thinking out loud through conversation. Many a husband has made the mistake of hearing his wife complain about something, only to be shut down when he tries to remedy the situation on her behalf. His thinking is straightforward and simple, "My wife has expressed an issue that is troubling her. I will come to her rescue and take care of the problem." However, when she hears his advice, she may become aggravated because she does not recall asking for help. As a result, both partners become frustrated.

After this happens a few times, that husband may assume his wife never wants his help. When a situation arises where she really would like assistance, she finds him "unresponsive." She feels disappointed and unsupported while he is bewildered and feels like he can't do anything right.

I remember in my early years of marriage expressing my hopeless feeling in this situation to an older married friend of mine. I'll never forget his sage advice. "Jerry, when she starts in on this conversation, just ask her one simple question: 'Is this something that you would like me to fix, or am I just supposed to listen?'" While I understood the logic in this, I thought it sounded terribly insensitive to actually ask. I was already struggling in this area, the last thing I wanted to do was aggravate Tara with such a question.

Within a few days, Tara came home from work in a terribly frustrated mood. She was upset at her boss and coworkers over some situation she had faced during the day. A few minutes into the conversation, I formed an opinion of how she could respond to overcome this problem. But before I could interrupt her with my advice, I remembered the words my friend had offered. When she paused to gather her thoughts, I asked her directly, "Is this something you want my help on, or do you just want me to listen?" I was amazed at her reaction. She cocked her head, thought for a moment, and responded with "I just need you to listen. Thanks." And she went right on with her story as if I'd never interrupted her. She wasn't offended at all. In fact, she seemed to appreciate me asking the question. At that point, my mind wandered, and I admittedly began to grunt the occasional *uh-huh* as she spoke. But even that was okay. As it turns out, she was mentally processing her situation as she verbalized it. I gave her that audience, and it satisfied her *more* than if I had given an unsolicited opinion or solution.

That simple question has become natural for us. I no longer have to ask her the question each time. There are times when she'll say, "I really need you to step in and help me with this." In those instances, I engage in the conversation, ask a lot of questions, and do my best to alleviate her stress. Otherwise, I quietly listen and nod...

Making Time for Conversation

We live busy lives. Jobs, kids, church, and other social obligations consume a huge percentage of our available time. There will be days and sometimes weeks where communication between spouses is limited to "drive by conversations," where you cross paths as one is entering the house while the other is exiting. While these peak periods will occur, the key is not to allow them to become your new norm. If you stop and think about it, you probably schedule every obligation and family event on some type of calendar. You know well in advance the date and time of Junior's dentist appointment or Suzie's piano recital. There's no reason that we can't schedule time for conversation with our spouse. The reason this doesn't happen is that we take this communication for granted, simply assuming it will happen organically in its own time. Not scheduling it puts it at the lowest priority. When faced with a time crunch, the lowest priority always falls of the schedule.

I know what you're thinking. Scheduling conversation? That sounds terrible. You can probably picture the awkwardness. You and your spouse sit across the table, look at your watches, and say, "We have fifteen minutes to talk, so you start." It doesn't have to be this way. There are other ways to prioritize communication that are far less rigid.

I spoke in an earlier chapter about Martini Mondays. That's a great, intentional practice, but there are other habits you can create. Make it a point to talk for ten minutes when you both get home from work. There's power in the "how was your day?" question, especially when you take time to listen to the answer. Pillow talk (that time between when you go to bed and when you fall asleep) is a great time to reflect on your day. If you both happen to be morning people, a chat each morning over coffee can be invaluable. Find a time that works for both of you and give it priority. You'll find that in a short while, you will come to look forward to that each day.

Summary

Effective communication is a challenge in most marriages. Like the other topics covered in this book, the best way to overcome it is to be intentional and focus on making it better. You and your spouse communicate differently. One may be more talkative and the other very quiet. Figure out what works for you and proactively communicate in that manner. Don't expect your spouse to read your mind, and don't offer solutions that aren't being requested. Remember, a message not received is not communication. Set aside regular time to have quality conversations where distractions are minimal. Be a good listener.

Discussion Questions

- On a scale from one to ten (ten being the best), how would you rate the communication in your marriage? How does this compare with the score your spouse gives?
- How often do you say things to your spouse that you later regret? What could you do to reduce or eliminate this?
- What is your biggest frustration in terms of communication with your spouse?
- Do you currently take the time to have regular, uninterrupted conversation? If not, is there some way that you could arrange that?
- What rules of engagement could you put in place to improve communication in your marriage?

LEADER'S STUDY GUIDE
FOR SMALL GROUPS

Leader's Study Guide

Marriage enrichment is a commonly desired study topic for small groups in churches. This section is written as a guide to be used for such groups. Whereas the questions at the end of each chapter were intended for couples to answer together, this section will provide additional questions (of a less personal nature) that can be comfortably discussed in a group setting.

As a group, determine how many sessions you would like to spend covering this book. As an example, if you choose to do a single chapter a week, it would take you ten weeks to cover all of the material. If you would like to complete it sooner than that, you can combine multiple chapters into a given session.

If you wanted to complete the study in six weeks, I recommend you combine chapters 1 and 2 (shocking marriage, building a foundation), chapters 6 and 7 (keep the spark alive, intimacy) and chapters 8 and 9 (outside influences and modeling).

Decide on the duration of your study in advance so that you can assign the reading to your group prior to each meeting. That will allow you to use the following group discussion questions at each meeting.

Establish Trust

It is important to stress with your group you will be discussing topics over the course of this study that may be of a sensitive nature. Ask the group to agree to not share any comments made during your sessions outside of the group. It is critical that people feel *safe* in sharing thoughts and concerns within your group. Remind them multiple times over the course of the study, especially once sensitive information has been shared by someone.

Format

Facilitate your group discussion in whatever format works best for you. The following is a suggested guide I have used when working with groups.

- Open each session with prayer. Pray specifically for the couples in your group and ask for God's blessing on each marriage represented there.
- Discuss any updates from the prior week's prayer requests.
- Encourage couples to share any learning, insights or "aha moments" they may have uncovered during their reading and discussion of the material.
- Promote an atmosphere of transparency. Lead by example - share your own answers first. You want couples to be able to share areas in which they may be struggling or in commitments they want to be held accountable to. Ask the couples if anyone wants to share any of the answers they came up with at the end of each chapter.
- Once you get to chapter 3, encourage couples to share any rules of engagement they have created within their own marriages. Continue to do this for each subsequent week. You will find that other couples will benefit from this, and it may spur them on to create similar rules for themselves.
- Go through the following group questions. Have multiple people answer each question. Encourage discussion and debate. Help the group to go beyond superficial answers to share personal stories or opinions where applicable.
- At the end of each session, ask for prayer requests. Ask how the group can hold up each marriage in terms of their specific challenges or struggles.
- Assign reading for the next session.

Chapter 1: Shocking Marriage

Questions:
- Describe the fanciest wedding you ever attended. What stood out about it?
- Describe your own wedding. What were the most memorable elements of it?
- Do you see a connection between the size/cost of a wedding and the long-term happiness of the couple? Why/Why not?
- In your own words, describe what the author means by a shocking marriage. What does a shocking marriage look like? Give specific examples of things you've personally seen.
- Why is having a vision for your marriage important?
- What does a couple have to do to create a shocking marriage?

Chapter 2: Build A Solid Foundation

Questions:
- Read Matthew 7:24–27 aloud.
- Who was Jesus talking to? What did he want his listeners to take away from His message?
- What does it mean to build your marriage on rock and not sand?
- The author shares his story of early married life built on sand, and how over time he came to re-build it upon rock. What was the turning point that helped him realize his foundation was fragile at best? What made him decide to rebuild on rock?
- Think about your own marriages. Are there elements to the author's story you can relate to? Share

them with the group.
- Describe in your own words God's design for marriage. How well is our culture aligned with this original design? Be specific.
- What are your thoughts on the Holy Spirit's role in marriage? What does this look like?

Chapter 3: Rules of Engagement

Questions:
- The author talks about the importance of being intentional in your marriage. What does this mean? Why is it important?
- What is the purpose of having rules of engagement? How should they be used?
- The author gives examples of biblical rules of engagement. Can you think of any others that are mentioned in scripture?
- What are the differences between situational and proactive rules of engagement? How and when might each be used? Give examples.
- Has anyone created any rules they would like to share with the group?

Chapter 4: Dealing with Conflict

Questions:
- Is conflict really inevitable in a marriage? Why or why not? (Proverbs 15:18)
- What role does pride take in generating conflict? How can it be recognized? How can it be dealt with? (Proverbs 8:13, Proverbs 16:18–19, 1 Corinthians 4:7)

- The author described the difference in "conflict styles" that he and his wife had coming into marriage. Can anyone relate with that? Please share your story with the group.
- When should you let an issue go, as opposed to raising it up? What does effectively letting it go look like?
- The author told the story of John and Sue and their misguided argument. Who can relate to that? Have you ever been in a situation when you weren't sure what you were arguing about? Can you share that with the group?
- Why is keeping a long-term perspective so important when you find yourselves in an argument? How can you ensure you are doing that?

Chapter 5: Weathering Life's Storms

Questions:
- Does everyone face trials? What does the Bible say about that? (James 1:2–4, 1 Peter 1:6–7, 1 Peter 4:12–13, John 16:33)
- How can we prepare for future trials? Does it make sense to do so? (Proverbs 3:5–6, Joshua 1:9, Psalm 34:19)
- Are there rules you could create based on trials you've been through in the past in your marriage?
- What can you do to help other couples that you know are going through storms?

Chapter 6: Outside Influences

Questions:
- Who are the people in your lives that have an influence on your marriage?
- How do others intentionally or unintentionally influence your marriage?
- How does our culture attempt to influence marriage? Think books, movies, social media, etc. Give both positive and negative examples.
- What are some practical ways to recognize that your marriage is being affected by outside influences? (Proverbs 12:26; Proverbs 27:9).
- What can you do to minimize the impact of negative influences that you are around? (Deuteronomy 13:5; 1 Corinthians 15:33).
- How can you incorporate positive examples or influences into your marriage?

Chapter 7: Keeping the Spark Alive

Questions:
- Describe some of the needs that you have beyond your basic physical needs such as food and shelter. How many of these can you satisfy on your own? Which can your spouse help to satisfy?
- Why are you typically more focused on your partner's needs early on in the relationship? Why does this attention shift back to yourself over time?
- Discuss the difference between comfort and complacency. Is comfort bad?
- How do things change relationally in a marriage once children come into the picture? How does this change as the kids get older? What are the dangers

of becoming a child-first-focused family?
- Why is planning regular time together so important in a marriage?

Chapter 8: Intimacy

Questions:
- What is God's view on intimacy? (Hebrews 13:4, 1 Corinthians 7:1–5, Malachi 2:15, Proverbs 5:18–19)
- What is the "honeymoon phase" of a marriage? Why does it fade over time? What takes its place?
- Why is control such an issue in terms of intimacy in many marriages?
- The author shared a very personal story of he and his wife agreeing to try an experiment for thirty days. Can any of you relate to that story? In what way? Were you surprised at their learnings? Is this an experiment that you would be willing to try with your spouse?
- Have you heard the women are like Crock-Pots, men are like microwave ovens analogy? What is your take on this? What do you think of the author's opinion?
- How should intimacy evolve over time in a shocking marriage?

Chapter 9: Modeling Your Marriage

Questions:
- How is your marriage a reflection of your faith to an observing world? (Titus 2861 2:7–8; Matthew 5:13–16; 1 Corinthians 11:1)

- In what ways can you demonstrate a Godly example of marriage to other couples? Be specific.
- What examples did you have from your parents that you want to replicate? want to avoid?
- Why is it important to provide a positive model of marriage to your children? What does that look like? (Proverbs 22:6, 3 John 4)

Chapter 10: Effective Communication

Questions:
- Why is what you say to your spouse so important? (Psalm 19:14, Psalm 37:30, Matthew 12:37, Ephesians 4:29)
- What barriers to effective communication do you face in your marriage?
- What practical steps could you incorporate to improve the quality of communication within your marriage?
- How well do you identify with the gender roles the author described in terms of communication style? Give examples.
- What are some ways that you could make specific time for conversation in your marriage?

ABOUT THE AUTHOR

Much more than just a marriage coach who doles out truth, Jerry McColgin is an involved friend who winsomely speaks truth into a couple's life by gently shepherding them into a place where Godly counsel, soaked in grace with a dash of humor, is given. He is a sought-out advisor by many couples regardless of their stage in life. Jerry is an author, coach and speaker who encourages couples to have the type of incredible and unique relationship that God intends them to have.

Prior to being ordained as a marriage minister, he lived life as a corporate executive, an entrepreneur and a business consultant. He is the founder of Shocking Marriage Ministries, a group dedicated to fighting complacency and creating lasting intimacy in marriages. Jerry has been married to his beautiful wife Tara for nearly forty years. They have four children and nine grandchildren.

To learn more about Shocking Marriage Ministries (marriage coaching, blog, podcast) or contact Jerry about speaking to your organization visit the website at www.shockingmarriage.com. Also, join the Shocking Marriage group on Facebook to engage with other couples on relevant marriage topics.

Other Books by Jerry McColgin

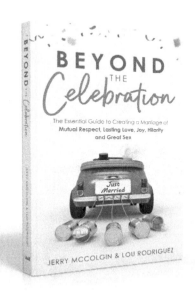

5 Star Reviews on Amazon

"McColgin and Rodriguez expertly lay out a workable plan for a long-lasting and fulfilling marriage, as well as list all the conversations engaged couple should be having NOW as they approach their wedding day... Their counsel on all subjects is clear, attainable, and enjoyable to read. This is truly a book in which all engaged couples can grow." J. Roberts

"This book is like a "Operator's Manual" on marriage, filled with very practical and valuable, but not commonly known insights about marriage... a must read for any considering a marital relationship." L. Erickson

"...As a licensed Marriage & Family Therapist for over 26 years, I can attest that this book would be a valuable asset to read as a couple planning for marriage, as well as those already married. A great book - grateful for it!"   S. Livingston

"Although this book is specifically designed for those not yet married, it is practical for all marriages, from those thinking of marriage, the married veteran and even the divorced. McColgin and Rodriguez ask questions every couple should be asking and provide the answers from a Biblical perspective. The topics covered (from expectations, finances, sex and in-laws et al) are thorough and refreshing. An absolute must for every couple!"   S. Teichmer